PRAISE FOR LEAD LIKE LOUIE

Danise and Louie have the ideal bond between human and dog—unconditional love. I have the same connection with my little dog, Joy, who not only brings me joy but also helps me be a better person *and* a better leader. Read this book and you'll see why it's no accident that *God,* spelled backwards, is *dog.*

—**Ken Blanchard,** coauthor of *The New One Minute Manager®* and *Leading at a Higher Level*

Who doesn't love stories involving adorable dogs? Danise has a unique way of taking heartwarming stories and moving them into lessons that are easily adaptable as tools to use within an organization. Our company has benefited from her use of these tools to improve our team's leadership behaviors. This contributed a great deal to the growth of our company and personal development of our associates.

—**Nader Masadeh,** President & CEO, Buffalo Wings & Rings

LEADership is an influence, and Louie sure knows how to influence! (Danise does a nice job too!) The LOUIE Leadership Model guides our LEADership workshops with high schoolers, emerging leaders, and those who have reFired (rather than retire). Understandable, actionable, and quite memorable. L is for Love, and LEADership is Love—we Love Louie, Danise, and the lessons we've learned.

—**Bob Pautke,** Executive Director LEAD Clermont Academy

Such a wise dog! Louie seems to understand human nature better than many humans!

—**Debbie Simpson,** President Multi-Craft

Lead Like Louie reminds me that leadership and doing the right thing are pretty simple—we humans make it complicated.

—**T.D. Hughes,** Former CEO and Chairman of the Board, LaRosas Inc.

Very timely and insightful advice. Louie and his mom are relationship experts and I always enjoy hearing about his adventures.

—**Patti Massey,** President MYCA Group

I was astounded with Louie's story and Danise's link to leadership principles. She was invited to lead a series of time slots for the Edoc Service staff. What a memorable story (still ongoing) and remarkable training.

—**Jim Mullaney,** President/CEO Edoc Service, Inc.

Lead Like Louie gives a fresh set of "eyes" for appreciating the direct connection between relationships and leadership, all through Louie's unique and entertaining perspective.

—**Chuck Proudfit,** President, SkillSource

LEAD LIKE LOUIE

lessons learned from a Rescue Pup

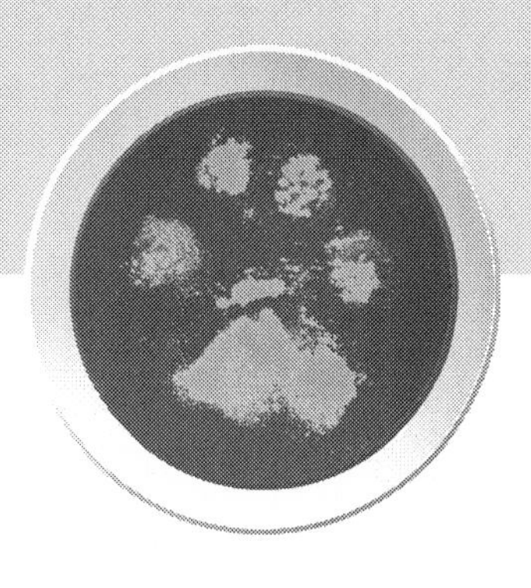

Danise C. DiStasi

Foreword by Mark Miller

ISBN: 978-1-7327067-1-2 (soft cover)
ISBN: 978-1-7327067-2-9 (ebook)

DiStasi Advisors
Loveland, Ohio
www.di-advisors.com

Original Blog Editor: Maryam Kubasek
Book Editor: Deborah Gaston
Cover and Interior Designer: Rachel Royer
Typesetting: Lori Weidert
Proofreading: Carrie Koens

Printed in the United States of America

This book is lovingly dedicated to Marisa and Matt.
You are such wonderful leaders to my precious grandchildren, Evi and Mea.

To Louie: Though you are considered a rescue pup, it is my *life that* you *saved.*

CONTENTS

Section Four
INVEST IN OTHERS 115

Section Five
EMPOWER OTHERS 147

FOREWORD

I'm allergic to dogs—seriously. If a dog walks into the room, I can be sneezing within two minutes. So, I may be the last person you would expect to write the foreword for Louie. But here is why it makes perfect sense to me…

Leadership is the cornerstone on which the future is built. Leaders, good or bad, will determine the destiny of our organizations, culture, country, and ultimately, the world. This simple truth is why I have dedicated my life to encouraging and equipping leaders. I am also committed to using any means necessary to serve leaders around the world. Granted, my methods have always been more conventional such as writing, speaking, international traveling, or posting on social media, all the usual suspects. However, I will confess, I never considered a canine angle—until now.

When my friend, Danise, told me Louie was compiling a book of her blog posts from the last five years to help leaders see the world from a slightly different (doggy) point-of-view, I knew writing this Foreword would be one more way I could encourage leaders!

Besides, there are approximately 55 million households who provide homes to the 90 million dogs in the United States. I'm sure the vast majority of you can relate immediately to the challenges, joys, and lessons to be learned from Louie's life and insights on leadership.

Consider how often we discover, or rediscover, a hidden truth by seeing it with fresh eyes. I'm guessing you've never looked at leadership from a dog's vantage point. I am hopeful that Louie's perspective, embodied in Danise's authentic, real-world experiences, will bolster your resolve to lead at a higher level.

Thanks, Louie, for your patience with humans! With your help, we can all grow stronger, be more loving, and become more effective leaders.

—Mark Miller, Best Selling Author,
Vice President of High Performance Leadership, Chick-fil-A, Inc.

INTRODUCTION

What does a dog have to do with leadership?

What does this picture say to you about leadership? Take a moment and ponder this beautiful scene before responding.

I've asked that question over the years as I have spoken in front of numerous audiences, and I continue to be amazed by the responses. This is not simply a picture of a little girl and her dog. This is a picture of life, love, leadership, and trust between my granddaughter, Evi, and Louie, my rescue pup. Here is a sampling of some of the responses I've received about leadership: they are on a path together; she is holding the leash in a relaxed, yet firm position; she is overseeing his walk; they are side by side; and he seems to be enjoying wherever they journey together.

Ah, the last point is the very reason I decided to write this book. What you don't see in this picture are the steep hills we climbed and descended, the brush we cut through with our arms, and the mud we waded through just to get to this leveled path—seemingly the most enjoyable part of the journey.

And although it seems that the path was the destination and goal, it was actually the uncomfortable and difficult journey that allowed us—myself included, because I took the picture—to enjoy this particular space together. Although it took Louie some time, he learned to trust us and, somehow, knew that no matter what the journey entailed, we would get him to our destination safely.

It is for this reason that we that invite you on this journey with us. It was not an easy one, yet there were so many hidden treasures along the path that we can look back on with joy and the promise of better leadership behaviors for others and myself.

Although I'd love to say this journey began with lots of warm, fuzzy feelings and puppy kisses, that just isn't true. The truth is that when I first adopted Louie, he displayed many challenging behaviors that made me question my decision to adopt him, yet something incredible happened once we engaged a dog trainer. I wasn't only learning dog-training techniques; I was experiencing leadership development through an entirely unconventional method that proved to be beneficial to Louie and me—and even more so for my clients.

As I shared stories of Louie's latest escapades with my clients, there was always a leadership lesson to be learned. The more I shared these challenging, yet sometimes funny and heartwarming stories, the more the lessons took hold within their entire organization. Why?

- The stories are memorable.
- The tools are applicable.
- The method is simple.
- The effectiveness is sustainable and replicable.

Louie and I journeyed together, yet I had no idea I was walking through specific stages of leadership. I wanted this dog to be fun, loving, and loyal. Many times that seemed almost impossible, but we persevered.

Once I looked back over the years, I saw a pattern in our lessons. And then I saw the stages unfold and a model emerge. We now have a straightforward and effective leadership model that helps individuals, students, and leaders at all levels to improve their leadership skills and behaviors, improve their engagement, increase productivity, and most importantly—enjoy life. This method is specifically designed to develop leaders to develop others.

We are pleased to share this model with you through heartwarming stories of courage and love, as well as techniques for overcoming common issues such as bullying, pride, fear, doubt, and numerous others—all seen through eye-opening experiences with my rescue dog.

I have refined all that Louie has taught me into a leadership model that is easy to remember and follow: the LOUIE Leadership Model.

This is not another cute little doggie book with a feeble attempt to share life lessons. The lessons are challenging and the stories are real. This book is a compilation of blogs written since Louie's adoption in 2013. You'll get the most out of this book IF you don't read it from cover to cover. You can decide which section you want to read first (though the model is sequential). The content is divided into five sections. Each section corresponds to the five stages of the LOUIE model. Every chapter within each section is a self-contained lesson with its own stories and leadership tools. Once you've completed the five sections, read through the Author's Note as it provides an excellent summary and tools to take a deeper dive.

Thanks to Louie, I've learned the real value of leadership, and our journey together has revealed how to successfully develop leaders. This simple yet effective model combines the leadership experience that I've had over the last several decades with extensive leadership research, and presents the most essential leadership requirements:

1. **L**ove, trust, and respect are foundational in leadership.
2. **O**bjectives and goals are needed to provide direction, strategy, and alignment.
3. **U**nderstanding others and ourselves is key to work through conflict.
4. **I**nvestment in building relationships and developing leaders.
5. **E**mpower and encourage your team to thrive and succeed.

Through *Lead Like Louie,* you will journey over rough terrain and through challenging issues. But you'll enjoy the path that helps you understand how your everyday behavior affects your relationships and your team's outcomes. And you'll learn ways to improve your effectiveness in your personal, community, school, and professional relationships. Share the learnings with your team, friends, and family. That's how we impact organizations and individuals, by developing leaders to develop leaders.

Enjoy the journey.

Section One

LOVE IS FOUNDATIONAL

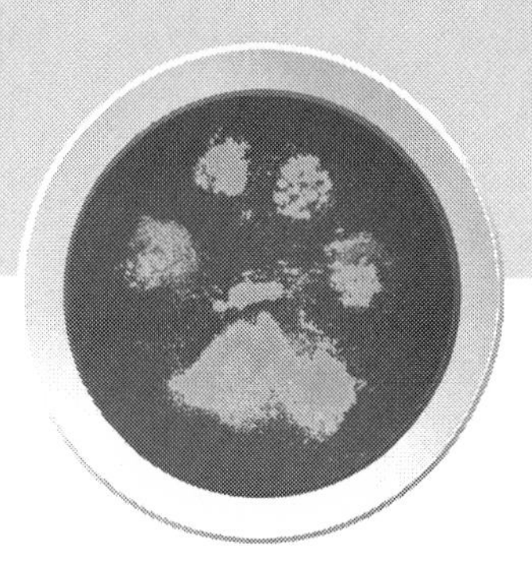

"To be loved but not known is comforting but superficial. To be known and not loved is our greatest fear. But to be fully known and truly loved is, well, a lot like being loved by God. It is what we need more than anything. It liberates us from pretense, humbles us out of our self-righteousness, and fortifies us for any difficulty life can throw at us."

—Timothy Keller

Louie was either lost or abandoned in Kentucky and made his way, through a number of shelters, to Cincinnati, where I live. Although I love dogs, I had decided not to get another one for many reasons—that is, until I just happened to stop by PetSmart while they were conducting an adopt-a-pet weekend and I encountered this abandoned mutt with big brown eyes. I tossed my concerns aside, brought him home, and named him Louie DiStasi. I soon discovered that Louie had brought a lot of emotional baggage to the relationship. He demonstrated behaviors that deeply concerned me, and I engaged a dog trainer to help address them. I quickly realized I needed training as much as Louie did, if not more so.

I'm not afraid of tough lessons, and I'm always looking for ways to improve my leadership skills. But working with Louie was challenging. The bottom line was that Louie needed acceptance, consistency, discipline, and—above all—unconditional love. I wasn't sure I was equipped to provide all that.

I loved Louie when he was a good little dog who was sweet and absolutely adorable. But I didn't love him so much when he started to act out and behaved badly when people came to the door, etc. It was a struggle, and I had to make a choice to love him. I decided to commit to loving this abandoned pup, in spite of his baggage.

Employees, friends, and other teammates can be like Louie. They bring a lot of baggage to the job or school and may be hard to love at times. One of the most critical needs for any human being is the need to feel loved. All of us have this innate desire, yet it is one of the most difficult to fulfill. In addition to Timothy J. Keller's quote at the beginning of this chapter, I often share this quote from Brené Brown:

> "A deep sense of love and belonging is an irreducible need of all people. We are biologically, cognitively, physically, and spiritually wired to love, to be loved, and to belong. When those needs are not met, we don't function as we were meant to. We break. We fall apart. We numb. We ache. We hurt others. We get sick."

Love is not merely a warm fuzzy feeling; love in action is the aspect that is important in leadership. When I mention the word "love" in the workplace, I receive a tremendous amount of pushback. People say, "Don't bring it up; you'll have HR issues." I question whether people understand what love really means.

While other people can be hard to love at times (maybe most of the time), you have a choice to make: you can choose to love, or be indifferent toward them. Let's look at the characteristics of leaders who love:

- They are patient.
- They are kind, not rude.
- They honor other people.
- They are honest.
- They are protective.
- They are trustworthy.
- They are always hopeful.
- They persevere through difficult situations.
- They are other-seeking and other-serving.
- They manage their emotions well.

Of course, there are also things that they are not:

- They aren't envious.
- They aren't boastful.
- They aren't prideful.
- They don't hold grudges.

The characteristics of loving leaders are those that leaders should display when they are working with their people—baggage and all. That's what love in action looks like.

Louie was transformed by the love I poured into him. I see this same transformation in others when I choose to be patient, kind, honest, and loving.

1.1

LEADERSHIP TRAINING DOESN'T WORK BUT LOVE WINS EVERY TIME

What does it mean to truly love and develop others?

Louie, my adopted pup, and I were walking down the street toward our home. A neighbor was getting into her car and stopped to smile at Louie as he proudly pranced by. We exchanged hellos, and she smiled at Lou and said, "He's such a good boy." I just laughed and nodded.

He looked at me and I at him, and I thought, "He is a pretty good dog." But then I continued that conversation in my head: "Well, most of the time. I mean, sometimes he can be a bit, well, let's just say mischievous." Quite honestly, he is a totally different dog than he was during our first few months together.

Louie's transformation was no accident—I was very intentional in making changes in my life and my leadership style, and it took a lot of work.

But the most transformative power in our journey together was my decision to be a loving person and to pour love into little Louie. I saw a significant difference in his behavior a few months into our time together, and continue to see today!

Sadly, the word "love" receives eye rolls and shoulder shrugs. The word gets tossed around frequently these days in every circle that wants to claim they are the most loving. We see countless hateful Facebook posts and counter posts on how we need to love. Some time ago, in my first *Louie's Leadership Lessons* blog post, I took a chance and wrote about showing Lou unconditional love, knowing how the world viewed the "l-word," especially in the workplace. Yet as we conduct more and more LOUIE speeches and workshops, one thing that is always consistent is the total misunderstanding of the word love.

A few months after my blog post on love, *Harvard Business Review*[1] published a study demonstrating that employees perform better when they feel loved. The study made a distinction between friendship love and romantic love, mainly that friendship love is based on warmth, affection, and connection rather than passion. The study revealed, "It is the small moments between coworkers—a warm smile, a kind note, a sympathetic ear—day after day, month after month, on a consistent basis, that help create and maintain a strong culture of companion love and the employee satisfaction, productivity, and client satisfaction that comes with it."

So here's my challenge to you today: Stop training and coaching your staff in hopes of seeing change. Be the leader who genuinely loves! Unless you're capable of showing authentic love to others, you will most likely cultivate a very toxic culture within your organization, family, and community. Don't confuse being nice with demonstrating love. They are two different qualities. Love is a heart issue!

On the flip side, my observation has been that bosses who try to manufacture these qualities but demonstrate behavior to the contrary engender fear and mistrust among their employees.

May I be so bold as to take this a step further? I think it is virtually impossible to feel joy or experience peace in your life if you're incapable of true, genuine love. Most of us do not understand love, so let me help you. Here's the tip of the iceberg of what I've been learning over several years of studying and blogging about Louie and love:

- Love is an alignment of the whole self toward what is good and right.
- Love must be aimed at and practiced. It takes work; as Martin Luther King, Jr., said, "It takes strength to love."
- Love is not turned on and turned off for this person or for that. It is consistently who you are.

---

[1]Sigal Barside and Olivia A. O'Neill, "Employees Who Feel Love Perform Better," *Harvard Business Review,* January 13, 2014.

- To demonstrate love, *be* a person possessed by love, so that you can go to an adversary as a loving person rather than going to an adversary and then trying to love that person.
- Love arises out of a pure heart.
- Love is directed toward what is good and right from the depths of ourselves, from which actions come.
- Love itself is patient, kind, trustworthy, and true; it is not prideful, doesn't hold on to grudges and is humble. We are to pursue love, and the rest takes care of itself.
- Seek what is best and what is true. Truth is sometimes very hard to share and to hear, yet many times it is the most loving aspect of a genuine relationship.
- Love is not something you choose to do, but what or who you choose to *be.*
- Look for the sources of malice in yourself and focus efforts upon grace to change them.
- Malice is rooted in how we think of people—as objects—with little understanding of who they are or the difficulties they may have experienced in their lives.
- Finally, love is the willingness to serve others for the greater good, above our own wants.

There's no way you can be patient with others, show kindness, have integrity, be faithful to your word, be gentle, or exhibit self-control without love. All of these excellent characteristics are rooted in love. And as leaders, we must be people of love, not just doers of nice things. Check your motives and your hearts.

It wasn't easy for me to show consistent, genuine love to Louie. And it has been even more difficult to show love to people who are unlovable, demanding, or different from me, or those who have disappointed me. But I know what true love is, and I stand amazed that God so loves me! Who am I to withhold that love from people who may need it most?

I chose Louie, difficult personality and all. Granted, we usually do not get to choose those we are commanded to love in the workplace, but people in your space could be transformed simply because you choose to love them.

1.2
STEP UP AND LEAD WITH LOVE

Be the strong, bold leader you were meant to be!

As I continued to learn to be a good leader to my rescue pup, Louie, and love him unconditionally, one of the toughest principles for me to grasp was how to be the alpha. That's right, and my trainer let me know that I was a weak alpha. My lack of strong leadership caused confusion for Louie, forcing him into the position of having to step up and lead.

Before Louie and I found each other, I never gave much thought to asserting my role as Alpha Dog. Consequently, my dogs assumed that role, and I let them. It didn't seem to matter because they were small and harmless. And by the time I got home after a long day at work, I was tired of being alpha, so I let them boss me around. But that approach doesn't work for Louie, and it does not work for people.

There is so much that goes into being a good alpha: being consistent, providing safety, setting appropriate boundaries, giving genuine and abundant praise, and offering a necessary correction. Again, all of those things must be rooted in trust and undergirded by love.

When the trainer first met us, Louie behaved very badly, and I was at my wit's end. The trainer described my body language as defeated. Body language is a powerful communicator. Like people, Louie noticed my tone of voice and body language, including facial expressions. Louie responded to my defeated body language with fear and confusion. The words from the trainer that moved me off the dime were, "I've seen you do leadership seminars, now you've got to do what you do in those workshops. Exude confidence. He needs reassurance that you know what you're doing."

Really? For my dog? I had made the common mistake of assuming that he would instinctively know that I'm the boss—simply because I'm the human, I'm larger than he, and I think more "knowledgeable." The trainer taught me that it is about my level of confidence in where I'm going and what needs to be accomplished. That confidence is in knowing what's best for Louie, giving him firm direction, and drawing out his very best behavior.

As leaders, our assumptions about others and situations around us unintentionally cause confusion among our team. We have expectations that are not always clearly communicated and then, when not met, cause disappointment on our part and confusion on the part of others. Ken Blanchard, author of *One Minute Manager,* often refers to this as seagull management, where a manager only interacts with employees when a problem arises. This style of leadership involves hasty decisions about things of which they have little understanding, resulting in messy situations for others to clean up.

Being a strong leader is about so much more than claiming an impressive title, wearing expensive suits, and appearing important. It is about:

- Being consistent. Good leaders (and good dog owners) are calm, controlled, and safe on a consistent basis. While it may feel like love to let Louie climb on my bed or turn my shoes into his personal chew toys, it is not. Good leaders give clear guidelines, set appropriate boundaries, and respect individual personalities.
- Owning the leadership role we've been given.
- Resisting the urge to react out of our fears and insecurities.
- Addressing problems before we lose our cool.

Dogs *and* people need a humble leader, not a bossy dictator. I've committed to leading with intentionality, clear vision, and goals. I encourage you to do the same—whether you're leading canines or humans.

I am happy to say I have assumed my role as alpha of the house, and consequently, Louie is a much happier pup. I had to wrestle him to the ground once or twice to make him understand submission, a method I do *not* recommend for your team, but it is clear that he understands and appreciates my love and leadership.

1.3 THE POWER OF FORGIVENESS

A necessary tool for servant leaders

I continue to be amazed at the communication skills of my pup, Louie. For not speaking a word, he is capable of relaying so many messages. His body language expresses happiness, playfulness, fear, anxiety, and most importantly, love.

One winter when we had a break in the weather, Louie and I took a long walk and enjoyed the fresh air, even though it was still quite cold. We went through our usual routine when we returned home: taking my boots off in the garage, wiping his feet, and having him come into the kitchen to sit on the area rug for a minute while I remove my coat, etc. He does really well with this process and is very patient.

I went on with my workday and, after a few minutes, I wondered why he had not followed me as he usually does. I came back into the kitchen and there was Louie, sitting perfectly still right by the garage door. I had forgotten to take off his leash and the handle was caught in the door. Rather than bark, fuss, and prance around, he waited…and waited. There was no look of anxiousness. In fact, his big brown eyes looked at me as if to say, "No worries, Mom. I forgive you!"

I know he's a dog and his life isn't as complicated as a human's, but one of the reasons Louie and most other dogs have uncomplicated lives is because they don't harbor grudges. They aren't weighed down by resentments like many of us. Even if they are abused, most dogs quickly forgive. Perhaps we could learn a lesson from that.

For those of us who seek to be servant leaders, forgiveness must be at the top of the list of characteristics and qualifications. A pattern of broken relationships and constant grudges are a red flag and a sign that something needs to change. Here are some things to consider if you see a pattern of unforgiveness or holding on to resentments:

1. It's not about you! A leader must be other-focused. When we make a mistake or hurt someone and it is brought to light, we must own our behavior and ask for forgiveness. A good leader doesn't seek to justify his or her mistakes.
2. When someone else has made a mistake and it costs us productivity, time or hurt feelings, the most freeing thing we can do for all parties involved is to forgive. Flippantly saying, "Oh, I forgive them in my heart," but then seething inside, and sharing the offense with everyone over and over again, only leads to self-imprisonment. Over time, this will cause physical, mental, and spiritual harm.
3. Work hard to not offend anyone while never compromising truth. Learn to communicate truthfully with a heart filled with love. Then when an incident occurs—and it will—it becomes easier to immediately forgive.

Every time I look into Louie's eyes I see, "You are loved and forgiven, Mom!" Indeed I am, Louie! Indeed I am!

>>>

YOU ARE LOVED AND FORGIVEN, MOM!

>>>

1.4 LIFE INCLUDES NECESSARY ENDINGS

I love the Christmas season for many reasons. It is a wonderful time to celebrate life, enjoy relationships, and look forward to a new year, which could mean a new "do over" if we felt the past year was tough. I especially enjoy taking time to reflect on what I would change and how I will strive to be a better person next year.

Added in the mix this year is my love for my crazy dog, Louie! This time last year, we had been together for a couple of months and were still figuring each other out. Now, I look at him and wonder what his life would have been like had we not met. We still have a lot of work to do together, but I believe he is so much better off today than he was this time last year.

I am also reminded of the relationships I no longer have. Louie would not be with me if I still had my sweet little Bichon, Cece. And what would life be like if my mom and dad were still alive to see my grandchildren? Both my parents have been gone for more than twenty years, yet I still miss them and remember clearly the Christmases we shared.

Our little Cape Cod home nestled in a suburban cul-de-sac brimmed with energy, beginning with Christmas Eve. We would have a large celebratory meal and all eight of us would pile into the Edsel to go to midnight mass. Afterwards, family and friends would come to our home while we kids were hustled off to bed so we wouldn't "delay" Santa.

We would awake predawn and run down the stairs. We realize now that our parents stayed up all night putting toys and bikes together to surprise us. With six children and a father who was an officer for Cincinnati Police Department, that was a magical feat in itself. But surprise us they did, and there was always a really "big" gift that would take our breath away at the end of our wrapping paper frenzy. Even our faithful dog, Smokie, would join in on the fun, discovering the dog treats my mom wrapped for him to uncover.

More family and friends would come over for a brunch that would last for hours. Once again, we'd pile in the car and head to our grandparents' home for another large meal and fun times. We sometimes stopped at an uncle's home and, once we kids called it a night, there were even more people who would come and visit with Mom and Dad.

I can't imagine how they did it all, but my mom and dad enjoyed life to the fullest, and I will always appreciate that about them. I honor their memories by celebrating Christmas with the same vigor, love, laughter, and life.

Sadly, life includes necessary endings. Saying goodbye to my parents, experiencing other tragic losses too painful to mention, and bidding farewell to one too many furbabies I've carried in my arms means I have closed the chapter on a part of my life, but am opening a door on another. Louie represents one more chapter in my life, and he brings me incredible joy. And each chapter just keeps getting better, as I've shared with my daughter Marisa. I've enjoyed every stage of her life, but I believe this stage is the best so far!

1.5 LOUIE NEEDS MORE THAN "LEAVE IT!"

What letting go really means

Louie is a huge fan of my son-in-law, Matt. He thinks they are best buds. I'm not sure how this little love fest began, but perhaps it has something to do with Louie feeling like he and Matt are guys' guys! Or that Matt usually has one of my grandchildren with him. But every time a truck roars down the street, Louie does back flips hoping it's his buddy, Matt, and then he whines when it's not.

I agree with Louie; Matt is indeed pretty special. We were having a conversation the other evening about the difference between the phrases "let it go" and "leave it." While my granddaughters broke out in song, Matt wisely and simply explained that "let it go" means you actually have something to release, while "leave it," means you haven't taken possession yet.

"Leave it" is a command I often use with Louie. When we're passing a dog he doesn't like, or when he thinks he needs to run from a cat, or he wants to rummage through a neighbor's garbage bag, "leave it" is a common command for dogs and seems to work pretty well. He immediately points his nose forward, continues prancing down the street, and leaves the matter behind.

There are other times when "leave it" just doesn't work. He can't leave the feelings of fear or frenzy behind. He huffs and puffs and focuses on whatever is disturbing him. I recognize that those times will take a little more direction on my part. I stand between him and the object, and make him sit and look at me, which is a command he immediately obeys. Sometimes, though, his eyebrows go up and his ears go back, indicating he's less focused on me and more on the source of his obsession. Occasionally I will offer a treat to get him to focus on me. The goal is teaching him that whatever has caused him unpleasant feelings in the past can no longer have control over him. Like humans, Louie has a tough time learning that lesson.

After one recent "leave it" incident, I reflected on Matt's wise words, my granddaughters singing the song, "Let It Go" and the hidden gems in the movie *Frozen*. In the movie, Anna, the youngest daughter of the Queen and King and little sister of Elsa, was accidentally struck by Elsa's ice powers. The family immediately took her to Pabbie, the leader of the trolls, who healed her and wisely explained that fear will always be Elsa's enemy. The family then went home and closed off all the windows and doors because they thought Pabbie meant *others* would fear Elsa's powers. But in reality, Pabbie meant it was Elsa's and her parents' own fears that would be the enemy. Elsa's fearful emotions controlled her and caused confusion and disorder. Sadly, she distanced herself from everyone around her, even those she loved. This is true for many of us, as well.

What was the remedy? An act of true love. Not the romantic, superficial type, but honest, genuine, selfless love. And the affable, lovable snowman, Olaf, displayed that love when he was willing to melt into a puddle because he put Anna's

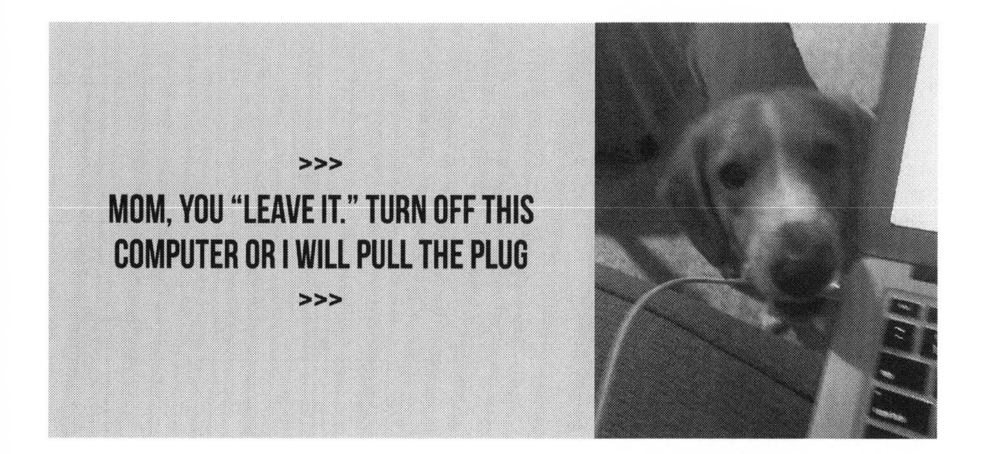

needs before his own. Fortunately, Elsa's icy heart melted because of her love for her sister, and it all ends well.

Good leaders notice when others may be steeped in fear or wallowing in angst over a situation. While a simple reminder to "leave it" may work, helping them focus on their strengths and on the positive parts of the project, and offering guidance and wisdom to persevere, is more effective.

Louie has learned that the command "leave it" means I love him, he can trust me, and whatever is causing him angst is not worth it. He has learned to focus on my gentle leading and when he does that, the irritation passes. But it requires more than words and simple remedies—it takes time, patience, love, and hopefulness.

1.6 WHAT IS IT ABOUT ALPHA GIRLS, LOU?

The balance between strong, bold, and humble

Louie loves his gal pals in our neighborhood, many of whom he would consider alpha dogs. Kaki and Ali were two of his favorites. There's Eve, who has no problem letting Louie know she has had enough of playtime. Ellie throws her paws around him and loves to run and play. And then there's Snickers, who used to turn her nose up at Lou, but now walks side by side with him.

I am the alpha of the alpha girls in Louie's world, and although there are times when Lou tries to exercise his independence, he is absolutely in love with me—and I with him.

My question is twofold. What is it about alpha girls that makes them so alpha? And what is it about them that has Louie so enthralled?

First, I'm not sure many women would deem themselves alpha girls. Yet many are, and although this is usually a good thing, it can sometimes be devastating. Over the span of my career, I have been blessed to know many strong women and have noticed an interesting phenomenon: few strong women, myself included, have truly achieved balance. I'm not talking about work–life balance or "integration"; it goes beyond that. There always seems to be something off-kilter that we, as women, want to straighten out or bring into balance, yet it eludes us.

But on this journey, if we remain diligent, there is a sweet spot that allows us to walk in harmonious balance: strength without being pushy, boldness without overpowering others, and humility without appearing weak. Every woman's quest for that sweet spot leads her on a journey of struggle and change, which can be difficult and yet incredibly freeing and rewarding.

So many times we stop just short of finding this sweet spot. A driving force takes over, and we feel that if we don't propel ourselves to the top, running over others along the way, then we simply will not survive. That's the lie many women today have bought into. I believe the antidote to being pushy, rude, and weak is simply love, joy, and peace.

- It takes *strength* to love others. Love is the ultimate test of strength. This is the deepest desire of every being, human and pets. When you truly love other people, you care more about them than you do about yourself. It is nearly impossible to be pushy with them. Instead, you care more about *serving*.
- When we think of *boldness*, we think of someone blasting on the scene, taking a stand, and being brave. Tip that boldness over the edge a bit, and you end up running over others and being rude. Joy is our elated response to experiences of life, even when life is tough. It is our response and deep satisfaction when we are able to serve others, not as an obligation, but because our heart prompts us to do so. When we have true joy in our heart, rudeness cannot emerge.
- *Humility* is the toughest characteristic to maintain, but once it is, inner peace is achieved. And when you're at peace, it doesn't matter if someone thinks you are weak.

I would like to see more women strive to balance strength, boldness, and humility by honing the character strengths of love, joy, and peace. We can do it!

As for *why* Louie loves alpha girls—they challenge him to be strong, brave (or bold), and fun (which equates to inner peace in Louie's world). One of his favorite alphas was his gal pal Ali. When she was outside, he could see her all the way down the street and would whine and pull to get a chance to dance around the

>>>

GLEANING WISDOM FROM MY FIRST PAL, EVE

>>>

front yard with her. She loved to play rough with Louie. He learned a little trick; he could stand just far enough away that her leash wouldn't allow her to reach him. His ears would go back, and he was on alert. She would stretch to get closer to him. Then, he would ease closer, and the dance would begin. He'd back up and then move closer—they truly enjoyed playing together. Ali challenged him to be a better, stronger, and more playful dog, and we are forever thankful.

Strive to walk in the balance of strength, boldness, and humility. Choose love, joy, and peace. In this sweet spot, you will impact others' lives for the better, thereby truly making a difference in our world.

1.7

DO UNTO OTHERS

What the "Golden Rule" actually means in our every day world

Louie is the perfect dog to lounge around with and enjoy downtime. One holiday season, we visited several friends and family members, and he was a perfect gentleman at each home. While visiting, I noticed something peculiar: He doesn't understand the Golden Rule.

We have a new friend in the neighborhood who loves to play with Louie. Claire Lee Himmel is an English Retriever and as rambunctious as they come. Though she is a bit larger than Louie now, she was much smaller when they initially met. She needed no introductions and ran right up to Lou, got right in his face, kissed him, pulled on his ears, bit his face, and jumped all over him. He didn't share her enthusiasm and backed away after giving her a quick snarl. He continued to demonstrate his disapproval as I stood talking to Claire's mom for a few minutes. This interchange took place every time we ran into Claire and her mom.

But when we run into his buddy Mick, a Golden Doodle, Louie behaves very differently. He runs up to Mick, grabs his ears, gets in his face, and nips at his legs until Mick calls it quits by sitting as close to his mom as he can get. Louie clearly loves to play the part of the bad little brother, giving little thought to how aggravating he can be.

Recently, we went to my brother's home to visit Louie's cousin, Noli Cannoli, a wisp of a dachshund, weighing every bit of five pounds but packed with 100 pounds of feistiness. She made it clear to Louie that he was to stay near me, he was not to walk around the home, nor get into any toys, go near his family or breathe, for that matter. Lou knew his place, sat quietly and behaved perfectly. All night he looked at me as though asking, is she for real? He slept all the way home, worn out from his cousin's energy.

But when one of his pals comes into our home, he does the very same thing Noli did. He immediately establishes the ground rules by his actions: Don't go in the kitchen, or go near my mom, don't look at any food, or in the direction of the pantry, don't drink from my water bowl or look out the window. I have to change the scenery and corral Louie and his pal into the family room to play and then suddenly, and it's all fun and games for Lou.

While I think his behavior is comical, I am reminded that we sometimes behave just like this. We want to be treated with love and kindness yet we pick and choose to whom we want to demonstrate those virtues. I am continually challenged when I read these words: "So in everything, do to others what you would have them do to you" (Matthew 7:12). The "Golden Rule" gives us a standard by which all of us who are naturally selfish people can assess our actions. This rule is a *positive* command to proactively demonstrate love.

It requires work and intentionality to treat others with love, patience, and kindness. It is easy to love the lovable or those who are just like us. But that's not what this directive requires. It is clear that we are to do to others what we would have them do to us.

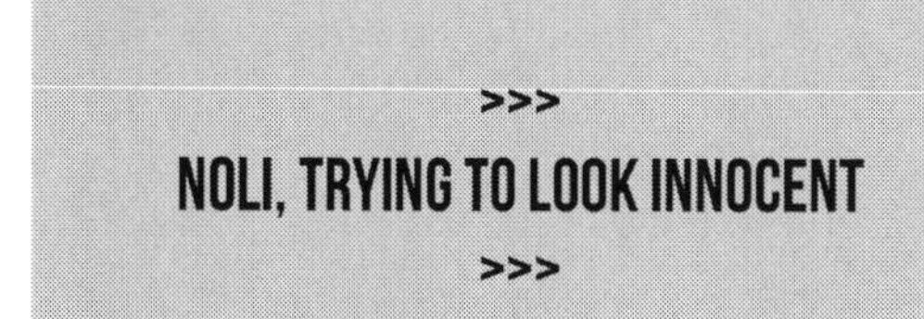
>>>
NOLI, TRYING TO LOOK INNOCENT
>>>

Many times if there is something that rubs us the wrong way about a person, chances are we have the very same quality that needs to be worked out of us. Think of this the next time you want to complain about someone. What is it about them that irritates you? Could it be that you display the very same quality? And if so, how can you treat that person as you would want to be treated? In the long run, it is not just about the other person, but it is working out a difficulty in ourselves. And the best place to start is by practicing the Golden Rule on a regular basis, whether we feel like it or not.

Louie will eventually get this—maybe. It is a very tough lesson for all of us to learn. It may take some practice with Claire, but now that she is bigger, he may grow to love her as one of his alpha girls. He loves alpha girls. Noli Cannoli will learn to love Louie over time, once she trusts that he will not get her toys.

My resolution is to be more intentional about treating others as I would want them to treat me, whether they reciprocate or not. I want this year—and every year—to be the year of intentionality and loving others.

1.8

A VERY SPECIAL GOODBYE

The power of love in an unloving world

Our little friend Ellie is lovingly featured throughout this book. But this chapter is dedicated to her as we lovingly remember our very special gal pal.

I knew this day would come. I had been dreading it for some time, yet I knew it was near. Louie's sweet little friend, Ellie, recently passed. Those who loved her, especially her mom, Lynne Ruhl, are devastated.

I met Ellie some time ago, when she was just a pup, while visiting with Lynne at her home. Ellie needed to be in my lap, next to me, by my feet, sitting right next to my chair—anywhere in close proximity. I wanted to believe I was special but as I grew to know Ellie, I realized she treated everyone pretty much the same. She just loved humans.

When my dear friend Lynne moved into my neighborhood, I was thrilled. Not only to have a close friend nearby, but also because of Ellie. I was able to spend more time with Ellie, walking her, having her visit with us. Louie loved her and often sought her advice, very much like I do with Lynne. (See Section Three—Addressing Conflict, with Ellie Ruhl.)

When her little face would pop up in the door window, I knew Lynne wasn't home. That gave me an opportunity to steal my little Ellie away and spend time with her doing our favorite pastime—walking. She was such a joy to walk. She pranced, like the princess she was. But the funniest part of walking her was when she would see a human. She was convinced that the person needed to see her, and she pranced right over to them. The person would light up when they saw Ellie, whether or not they were a dog person.

When she saw a dog, she would react the same way, convinced the dog was very much interested in making her acquaintance. When the dog showed signs of not wanting her near, she was shocked and unconvinced. I had to laugh at her desire to know everyone. I believe she thought if she loved all created beings, then all created beings would love her.

Oh, my sweet Ellie, if only that were true. If only our world loved as easily as you did.

Ellie broke her foot shortly after moving into their condo. She was running in the backyard and her foot caught in a grate. I thought she would lose her prance, but she seemed to spring right back. There were many long walks and fun times with that precious girl.

And then, over the last year or so, I noticed her decline. She slowly stopped jumping high in the air when she saw people, her prancing slowed—a little at first, and then a lot—and her long hesitation before hopping onto a step was noticeable. My heart was sad, and I looked for any sign of the precious little Ellie that I knew and loved. I usually witnessed an ever so slight indication, which thoroughly convinced me she was fine.

That was until I her took outside for the very last time. In fact, I knew it would be the last time I'd see her. I helped her up the step into the house. As she oriented herself, I knelt beside her. Not wanting to upset her with my display of emotion, I quietly whispered, "Ellie, you are loved. Thank you for loving me and Louie and everyone you came in contact with." That was all I could get out. The sadness was overwhelming.

I saw Lynne when she arrived home from Ellie's last visit with the vet. My heart broke for her because I know that pain all too well. Losing our pets is very difficult. Losing Ellie was heartbreaking for Lynne.

Honestly, I doubt I will ever meet another created being who could make someone—anyone—feel as loved as Ellie did. She exuded love and never cared who you were, what you did, or how you looked. If you were breathing, she loved you. Imagine our world if we treated others as Ellie did. And as much as I know

many people love Louie, I'm being truthful when I say he is a bit more reserved about showing love to others.

To our little Ellie: thank you for bringing such love into our world. You are sorely missed, little one. And you will always be loved.

"You, LORD, preserve both people and animals." Psalms 36:6

Section Two

OBJECTIVES AND GOALS

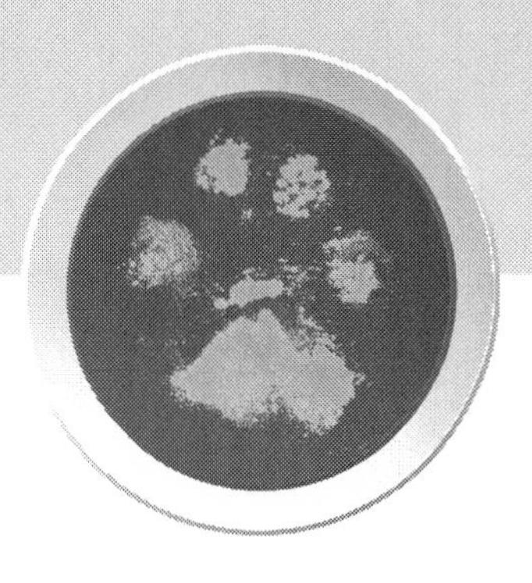

"What you get by achieving your goals is not as important as what you become by achieving your goals."

—Zig Ziglar

As our journey continued, I knew early in the game I needed help, so I engaged a dog trainer. The trainer, Zig, asked what did I want to achieve with training the dog? I thought that was a funny question. I just wanted him to be a good dog, fun to be around, loyal—like most dogs.

That was a great over-arching objective. But I quickly learned I had two very specific goals under that objective. Zig taught me that my first goal in this journey with Louie was to establish my role as leader. Yep—I actually had to learn how to be Louie's alpha. I wrongly assumed he would know I was in charge because I'm bigger than him, I own the house, and I pay for the meals. Assuming people will look to us for leadership just because we have a title or role in an organization is a mistake many leaders make.

The second goal I had to learn was that though I had a tremendous amount of knowledge about leadership, I had to be trained and developed in how to work with this dog. Again, we assume because we may have experience, we can rest on our laurels.

Throughout this section, you'll read the importance of objectives and goals with each lesson I learned by being with Louie.

2.1

SAFE AND SOUND

The number one objective: Build a culture of trust

We usually express a deep sigh of relief when we hear the words "safe and sound" from a loved one. The term is actually a Naval insurance term. Whenever a ship returned from a journey overseas, if everyone were "safe" it meant there were no injuries or deaths. The ship was "sound" if it had not suffered serious damage. So it is with Louie.

When Louie settles in for the night, I love on him, and invariably I hear his "safe and sound" sigh. His being content and safe is largely due to my consistent loving and firm behavior. He never has to guess how I am going to respond. He has learned that a certain behavior from him will evoke a certain response from me. I don't let bad behavior persist and then pounce on him. I am consistent with his discipline and even more so with his rewards. Because of this, he feels safe and is responding very positively to his new environment.

Consistency doesn't mean we are robotic. Louie loves variety and enjoys a new adventure or a new path to walk. And the point isn't simply to be consistent. Anyone can be consistently bad! The point is to be consistently good. For the sake of this book, let's stick with the good: my consistent behavior should always move Louie toward being a happier dog who loves his mama and his home! And so our leadership behaviors must be consistently moving our team toward having more trust, being more creative, experiencing contentment, and being more productive.

<<<
FEELING SAFE RIGHT NEXT TO MY ALPHA
<<<

It is next to impossible to trust an inconsistent leader. Their employees continually walk on eggshells because they never know if something is done perfectly, or if their very best effort will ever be good enough. An inconsistent leader may preach values but proceed to gossip about someone. An objective all leaders should have is to consistently display behaviors that promote trust and a safe culture.

I can certainly look back over the years and recognize that my own inconsistent behavior made it very difficult for people to be around me, much less for them to be content, happy, creative, and productive employees. I've also had a number of bosses who were very inconsistent with their behaviors. The mood was always, "do your job, keep your head down, and don't do anything to rock the boat." On the contrary, consistent behavior that builds trust means remembering the following:

1. Be who you say you are. People want to see you live the values you talk about.
2. Being inconsistent does not necessarily show up in an explosive temperament. Inconsistency can also be demonstrated through passive aggressive behavior.

3. Be open to change. A safe person is not afraid of constructive feedback. Model a willingness to work on your weaknesses. Your team just might follow your example.
4. Be open and transparent. When we are guarded, people suspect we have something to hide. On the other hand, don't go overboard on sharing personal data in an effort to prove you don't have anything to hide! Be genuine and discerning.
5. Have fun, lighten up, be consistently joyful.

We will achieve more when we set an objective to be consistently excellent leaders.

2.2 THE GOAL OF BEING PRESENT

Be aware

Confession time: I'm a multi-tasker and have trouble focusing on one thing at a time. In fact, I was one of those kids who received the checked box next to the comment, "Does not concentrate on task at hand," on almost every report card throughout grade school.

To this day, I justify my struggle with focus by saying I am a very creative person and I need to live experientially and savor the richness of the world around me in order to be a better writer. However, I understood very early in life that if I did not learn to focus I would be in trouble. The only nun who was impressed with my creativity was my English composition teacher. The others—not so much. So I became very intentional about focus and it has paid off.

Which brings us to Louie, who shares my struggle with focus. I shared with our trainer that he seems a bit skittish when I walk him in the dark, and he has a hard time focusing on what he needs to do while we're outside. The trainer reminded me that I am alpha, which means confidently leading Louie in a way that is fun and gives him safe freedom to do his thing, despite the darkness.

One beautiful morning, right before dawn, we walked a little further than normal and were moving at a pretty good clip. Since there was no one else around to whom Louie could react, I decided to check emails on my phone. In a flash, Louie jerked to the left, my phone went flying and three large creatures ran in front of us. They were harmless deer but they definitely startled Louie—and me. The deer moved on, but it was a few minutes before my heart stopped racing and

Louie settled down. As I picked up my phone, I had to shake my head. I know better than to check email, walk the dog, and pay attention to my surroundings simultaneously. Walking Louie only takes a small chunk of time each day, and he deserves my undivided attention—especially when we're walking in the dark.

And so it is with our teams, loved ones, friends, and people in general. Yet we pay so little attention to others, and rarely give them our focus and undivided attention. We sit in restaurants on our phones, checking Facebook or seeing if we received that "important" text or email. If we are attentive, it is usually because we want to get our point across as soon as that person stops talking. Let's face it, sometimes it's easier to carry on "virtual" conversations than it is to fully engage in real ones.

There is no greater gift we can give someone than to be fully present. People long to be known and understood. And the best way to know someone is to intentionally focus on what they are saying by not only hearing their words but also hearing their heart. It takes time and effort to truly "hear" people, yet it is the best way to demonstrate that you value and honor them.

At the time of this writing, we were celebrating Christmas. What better time to practice being fully present with whomever you're with? Take some time to truly focus on those around you. Be intentional, put down your phone, step away from the technological noise, listen to their words, and pay attention to what

their hearts might be saying. We've been given the best gift humanly possible through the birth of Christ. He modeled how to connect deeply with others. I often remind myself of that as I sit across the table from someone, walk through Findlay Market, or take Louie on a walk and say hello to neighbors that I only see occasionally throughout the winter months. I am intentional about locking eyes with others, not because I learned this in a business course or from the latest new leadership guru, but because people matter to God and therefore matter to me!

The best life goal you can set is to *be* intentionally present with others.

2.3 MEET THEM WHERE THEY ARE

Not everyone is on the same development track

Louie and I had arranged to meet Zig, our trainer, and his dog Deliah at a dog park one crisp autumn morning. Deliah is every pet owner's dream—obedient, well behaved, and playful. By contrast, Louie usually spent his time at the park scouting out the surroundings, greeting new dogs entering the park, and trying to get his hair to stand up so he would appear larger than he is. Besides Louie and Deliah, there were two other dogs and three of them were running and jumping, while Louie was marking every tree in sight, sometimes two or three times, making sure everyone would know he had been at the park.

Every once in a while Louie would start running and, invariably, get the other dogs to chase him. He is incredibly fast and very agile and usually very tough for other dogs to catch. But after a good run, he would go right back to marking trees and inspecting the fence to see if there was any place to escape.

Zig decided to throw a ball for Deliah to catch, hoping Louie would jump in on the fun. He'd throw the ball, Deliah would chase after it, and then bring it back to present it to her master. They did this routine over and over again with little to no attention from Louie.

Finally, Zig told me he was going to throw the ball right at Louie to see how he would react. The ball breezed through the air, bounced on the ground and gently tapped Louie right in the chest. Louie stood there looking as though there was something wrong with us. Why would we throw a ball at him?

Zig crossed his arms and said, "I am amazed. I have never seen anything like this. This poor dog doesn't even know how to play." I thought to myself, that's crazy. Every dog knows how to play, right? It's innate—they just play! Surely he knows how to play, he just chooses not to.

But after several attempts to engage him in playful activities that most dogs love, I had to agree that Louie simply didn't know how to play. I had assumed, wrongly, that playing comes naturally to all dogs.

Leader, isn't that just like us? We assume that a title or a certain amount of experience guarantees ability. But while a person may be capable, there are other variables (new job, new organization, new leader, new school or grade, new goals, etc.) that may impact their need for more direction. Here are some tips to help you avoid making assumptions that could hinder productivity and relationship.

1. Don't make assumptions; be willing to learn about others.
2. Understand where people are in their ability to do the task.
3. Give clear directions, ask questions, and check in to see how their progress is going.

4. Invite them to ask questions to ensure mutual understanding.
5. Learn to be a Situational Leader (The Ken Blanchard Companies, SLII®); fine tune your leadership behavior skills and provide the help your team needs to develop into top performers.

Surprisingly, Louie needed to learn to play. After working with him for some time, we now play fetch and wrestle a bit (until he opens that big mouth of his to engulf my entire head), and he loves to play with my neighbor's dog, Eve. I met him right where he was and he is developing nicely into a fun loving dog…who loves to play!

Make it an over-arching objective to give grace to others. This allows them to enjoy who they were created to be and they will be more open to being developed, when the time is right.

2.4 ME AND YOU AND A DOG NAMED LOU!

The goal of building a team

Louie needs a pack. He needs other four-legged buddies, and the more the merrier. He loves to play and frolic and just romp around because he truly enjoys being with other dogs.

However, it wasn't that long ago that he displayed signs of fearfulness and timidity and wouldn't engage in playful behavior with others. But as he has become an emotionally healthy dog, it is clear that he loves being part of a pack, which may consist of me, another dog, and maybe one or two other humans. His relational skills have increased tremendously and he is thoroughly enjoying life, not just surviving.

Why? Because he lets his need for others be known!

We've all heard the phrase, "We're better together." This is true for canines as well as humans. Here are some of the benefits Louie gets from being part of a pack:

- He's learned to negotiate when is the right time to take a chew toy from another.
- He watches, listens, and learns from others what level of roughhousing is acceptable to them.

- He learns how to problem solve by pulling a toy from the pile when another dog has his favorite.
- He shares—what's not to love about the communal water bowl?
- He's learned to resolve *some* "differences." When one of his buddies is done playing, they let him know. He usually pays attention, though sometimes he's like a bad little brother who finds joy in annoying others!
- He's committed and cooperates with others, especially on walks. He'll let his friends know if he's picked up a particularly interesting scent.
- He encourages others! This could be mistaken as whining, but by other's reactions as he runs to greet them, I believe this is Louie's way of singing… "Because I'm HAPPY; *wag* along if you feel like happiness is the truth!"
- He acknowledges and appreciates other's strengths—we're still working on this one.
- And finally—Louie loves Alpha Girls!

Louie continues to show me what it takes to be a great leader. Teams and relationships are necessary for our growth—we *are* better together. Appreciating and valuing what others bring to the table regarding ideas, energy, and connectedness is invaluable. Shutting down creative ideas because they are out of our comfort zone or because we didn't think of them first will stagnate not only the team, but also our personal growth.

Ken Blanchard says, "None of us is as smart as all of us!" We were created to be together and we go further with other people. And who knows? When we are intentional about being part of a team or a collective body of others and are open to their ideas, we may actually learn something.

2.5

NO ONE LIKES TO BE TOLD WHAT TO DO

From Louie's point of view

I am trying to say this in a nice way, but I'm just going to put it out there... no one likes to be told what to do. I know I'm a dog, and my leader mom is my alpha, and she regularly trains and gives me commands, but sometimes I just don't like being told what to do.

By now I know what makes my leader mom happy—walking beside her, letting go of something I shouldn't have, etc. Or my favorites: stay, heel, and down! But there are times when I know what I'm doing and she will give a command. And when I look at her as if to say, "I already know this," she sternly repeats the command as though I didn't hear her. So I decided to observe how some of my gal pals handle being told what to do.

First, there's Eve. When we took her outside, she was halfway down the sidewalk when my mom said, "Eve, don't pull." Then there was Ellie, who was already at eye level before her leader mom told her not to jump! Ali's been told not to kiss me so much but she never pays attention to that command. Khaki's been told by her leader mom to stop barking when I pass her house. That never works so I have to go give her some attention. And, of course, there's Snickers, who clearly doesn't like me, no matter what her mom tells her!

My buddies are not much better. My pug buddy Samson will walk in whatever direction he wants to walk, and Mick—well, Mick actually does what he's told.

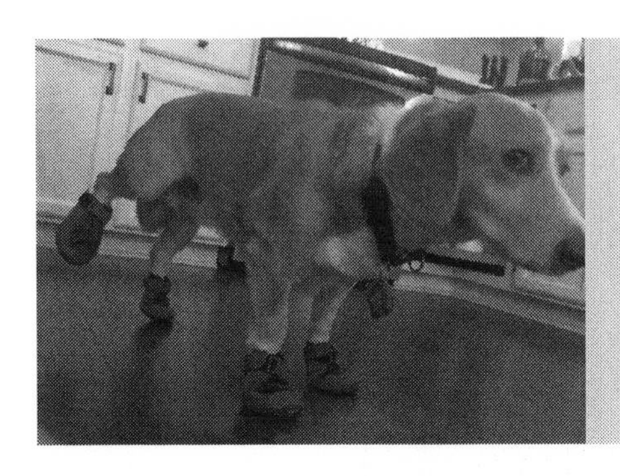

<<<

I DO NOT LIKE BEING TOLD WHAT TO DO

<<<

So six out of seven of my pals do not like being told what to do, which I believe proves my point.

But I decided to dig a bit deeper. I observed my leader mom as she read through several articles, such as *Five Things Successful Entrepreneurs Do; 13 Things Your Stylist Won't Tell You; What You Need To Do To Be a Strong Leader; Four things a Leader Does First Thing in the Morning,* etc. Interestingly, I noticed my leader mom does *not* follow every single suggestion. In fact, by reading her body language I'd say she is overwhelmed by all the suggested ways to improve. It is clear to me that humans don't like to be told what to do, yet often the first words you read or hear are, "Here's what you need to do!" So I concluded my research and the findings are as follows: Humans like to give commands and opinions on how to do things better, but no one listens!

After all this work, I needed a break, so I danced and whined by the front the door to let mom know that now would be a good time for us to go for a walk—and she obliged. The sunset was beautiful, so we strolled leisurely rather than walking at our usual brisk pace. In a flash, I saw a cat run past, and I immediately ran the other direction. SNAP! My mom called my name, snapped my collar and said, "STAY," as she made me stand at attention beside her. Then a car went flying by, narrowly missing us both! My mom was expressing her thoughts a little more animatedly than usual while I was catching my breath. I could have died if my leader mom hadn't told me exactly what to do right at that moment. Good thing she didn't say, "Louie, I wonder if there is a better way to express your fear of cats?" I would have died while we had that nice little conversation.

Then it hit me! There are times when clear directions (commands, in my case) are needed; a time when the Socratic method is appropriate, and a time when simply listening is the most loving and effective method. Some leaders *only* use the questioning method and it feels very manipulative because you know you have to do what they tell you or your job is in jeopardy. Others never offer the opportunity for team members to develop critical thinking skills, or the ability to explore other options, when they just tell you what to do.

I've experienced my leader mom's ability to balance her leadership behaviors. She knows when to give direction and when to provide support, and many times she balances the two nicely. She knows when to ask questions and when to listen. (It doesn't hurt that she's an avid student of Situational Leadership®). The most effective leaders are those who size up the situation and provide goals and just the right amount of instruction and care. Leaders who only have one leadership style (which is often some form of control and manipulation), miss out on the very best their team is willing to give.

I think Henry Cloud said it best in his audiobook (yes, I listen as my leader mom gleans wisdom from her audiobooks). "Behavior changes occur when we are able to grapple with issues. When you provide context—by listening, sharing information and positive examples, setting expectations and consequences, creating a healthy emotional climate, and challenging them to do their best—they will figure it out and implement it. That is a lot better than just 'telling them what to do.'"[1] That takes time and discipline, and from my observation, some humans don't have the discipline and won't take the time for others.

Ultimately, I've come to realize that my leader mom knows best! I've come to love and trust her so my heart's desire is to please her—not because she tells me what to do—but because I want to serve her. While no one likes to be told what to do, most of us love to give to those we care about. And the best form of caring is service!

---

[1]Cloud, Henry. *Boundaries for Leaders: Results, Relationships, and Being Ridiculously in Charge,* HarperBusiness, 2013.

2.6 THE DYNAMICS OF CHANGE

It's the little things that make a difference

"Nonna, do you ever get sad because you live alone?" asked my sweet six-year-old (at the time) granddaughter. My life flashed before my eyes as I thought of going from being raised in a family of eight full-blooded Italians (we have since grown exponentially) to becoming a very busy single mom of an active child with lots of friends. I smiled and responded, "No, Evi, I'm never sad to be living alone!"

"Well, you're never really alone," she responded. "You have Louie to keep you company."

Ahhh, yes, and there's always Louie! I am very grateful for Louie, and our time together is increasingly rewarding for me. But I have noticed over the last couple of weeks that he has reverted back to some of his earlier unacceptable behaviors.

It all started with my noticing his unusually boundless amount of energy. We did our normal long walks and he had play dates with his friends. But he was still anxious for more activity. While tossing the ball to play fetch one evening, I started wrestling with him—all in fun, of course (I can just see his trainer, Zig, shaking his head). While this may seem small and insignificant, this activity had ramifications that became clear.

The next morning I was working when I noticed my pup had slinked off to another part of the house. I went upstairs (and not quietly so he heard me approaching) only to find him nicely nestled on my bed! He didn't budge when I

noticed him although he clearly saw my body language and heard my expressive tone. He just looked at me with those big brown eyes as if to say, "Hey mom!"

"Get off that bed, now!" I said and with that he jumped off, and laid on the floor, belly up. Okay, sweet dog, let's just get back on track, I mumbled to myself. A few hours later, I was in the kitchen and when I went back downstairs, there was Louie sitting on my couch. Now, my dog is not allowed on the furniture, the one exception being a love seat on which he is allowed to sit and look out the window. That's it. This was only the beginning. Other odd behaviors started happening. He wouldn't walk alongside me, and he was constantly pulling to get ahead of me. I caught him a few more times on my bed, and he would rebelliously linger when I would say, "Here." Has he entered adolescence so soon, I asked myself? What on earth is going on with him?

And then it hit me. Ken Blanchard and his team have long taught on the dynamics of change. One dynamic is that when the pressure is off, we revert back to our original behaviors. Couple this with the fact that research shows it takes 21 consecutive days to form a habit and for a new course of action to be ingrained into a natural pattern of behavior. At first I reasoned that I was *long* past the 21-day mark with this dog, and he should be getting it by now. But then I asked myself if I had been consistent with my modification training for 21 consecutive days, or did I see improvement by week two and decide to ease off? I had to admit that I had taken the pressure off long before the 21 days.

And while this may seem unremarkable, I should have remembered that wrestling with Louie is a no-no. We were playing like he plays with his dog friends, and I am not his dog friend. I am his alpha. That behavior led him to believe we were on equal ground, and that he had full permission to sit wherever he wanted. Because the pressure was off, he didn't think I was serious about the behavior modifications, and he reverted back to his original behavior.

Isn't that just like us? We see a little improvement, and we slack off on holding ourselves and others accountable. We do this in exercise programs, healthy eating, sleeping enough, managing people and projects at work, and in nurturing our relationships. To make it worse, we often not only ease off, but also we latch onto the latest and greatest leadership idea. And we never really stay with the course of improvement we've started and for which we have asked others to hold us accountable. The best gifts mentors and leaders can give to others are both encouragement *and* accountability. Even more important is to press through, especially during the times when things have improved enough and you think you can slack off. That is the time others need you most.

Louie and I had to go back to the basics, review our goals, and stick with the program. He needs a leader mom who will stay the course and lovingly keep enough pressure on to see him experience the behavior change needed to live a happy life! As I'm writing, he's lovingly staring at me with his big brown eyes, as if to assure me he is never too far and always has me in his sight—and for that, I am truly grateful.

2.7

LOUIE, THIS IS A FOOTBALL!

Back to the basics

Based on Zig's advice, I enrolled Louie in Queen City Dog Training Club. I did so because, if all goes well, perhaps he can get into agility training at some point.

I filled out the online form and was hoping for an opportunity to share more detail on Louie's issues, but that would have to wait. I received a call requesting that I attend the first class alone, without Louie. I wondered why I needed to go to obedience training *without* Louie. I immediately started down the path of, "I am not the one with the issues. He needs to get started as soon as possible and I should not waste any time learning the rules of the game."

But off I went to the class, with about 12 other dog owners. As we filled out our papers, I finally saw my opportunity to share more about Louie. There was a very small space on the paper to express my concerns, which I completely filled and added additional comments in the side margins, but my anxiety level increased as I listened to others talk about their dogs.

I let out a long sigh as I pictured Louie in the training ring with other dogs that were much bigger and had even more problems than Lou. I wasn't sure I was up for my one night a week session with crazy Louie, who will no doubt be crazier with several other dogs with similar or worse issues. What was I thinking? It is *obedience* class. Perfect dogs do not attend obedience class. It is mostly dogs who have issues…like Louie! And the trainer made it clear: this is not a time of socialization, this is for obedience. Oh boy—here we go!

As stressful as the first session was, the obedience class provided ample opportunity for me to learn a few leadership lessons:

- First, when I returned home, I practiced the basics with Louie using his favorite treat—mozzarella cheese. He did really well. I was reminded of one of my favorite lines by Vince Lombardi, "Gentlemen, this is a football!" I realized I needed to constantly reinforce the fundamentals with Louie.
- The next day, when my daughter, son-in-law, and grandchildren were visiting, Louie was scrounging around for crumbs. I made him sit on his bed by the window and wait until we were done eating. As I walked into the kitchen, he slowly slipped away from his bed and quietly made his way back to my family. I had to make him go back and sit on his bed several times. Some lessons must be taught repeatedly!
- And finally, as I was walking Louie with one of his girlfriends, Ali, her mom kindly suggested I be a stronger leader to Louie. She was absolutely correct. And Zig reminded me that Louie is a control freak and needs to know I am in charge. This is another one of those leadership lessons I'm still learning—the need to continually establish my authority with Louie.

Honestly, I sometimes grow weary of leading anyone or being in charge of anything, much less a dog who should obey my every command. But what a delight when I return to the basics with Lou, and he immediately gets it. Seeing his response encourages me to continue to drill the fundamentals and prepare for the next level. It is not easy and, at times, it is not fun. However, it is incredibly rewarding. The same holds true for parents and for leaders in the workplace. As a leader, I am committed to press through, once again, and each level gets easier with time.

No doubt, the obedience class was as much for me as it was for Louie. By the time you read this, Lou and I will have been through our first class together and, most likely, will have survived and be ready for class two. Louie continually provides good fodder for our writing projects!

2.8 FALSE EXPECTATIONS VS. REALITY

Make sure you clearly communicate your objective

Louie and I took a long walk the other day and ran into our neighbor, Cindy, and her dog, Eve. Cindy invited us into their home to let the dogs play and expend some energy. When we walked in, Eve expected a treat, because that's what they do after she's been on a walk, so Louie joined her in expecting a treat and both dogs sat perfectly still, anticipating their reward.

When Cindy accidentally dropped a dog biscuit on the floor, Louie immediately snatched it up and gulped it down. He then sat back down again next to Eve and waited for his treat. Cindy knows "Louie speak" and said, "Lou, you already had your treat."

Louie was shocked and replied back, "That wasn't a treat! That was an accident; you dropped it on the floor and I picked it up. See me properly sitting here? I should get a treat because I'm sitting, just as I have been trained!"

"Sorry, Lou!" Cindy replied. I'm not sure, but I think Cindy ended up giving him a treat because she can't resist his big brown eyes. But the initial look on his face when reality set in was classic.

Facing the difference between our expectations and reality is a tough lesson for all of us. We've all experienced this at Christmas. In our minds, we picture a Norman Rockwell image of a beautiful Christmas tree, a warm, crackling fire in the background, hot chocolate with a perfect dollop of whip cream, and presents stacked up to the ceiling. In reality, it's rarely like that. While I wanted to believe in Santa forever—dreamer that I am—I had to face the reality that Santa did not exist when I found the box that held my beloved Thumbelina doll in our TV room later on Christmas day.

We've all had expectations that a new job would turn out wonderfully, but a year later we must face the reality that it's not at all what we expected.

So are we setting ourselves up for disappointment by setting our goals and expectations too high? And if so, does that mean we are settling for less and not even trying to reach a higher bar?

Leaders run into this issue all the time with employees, and we also deal with these issues personally. I think setting high expectations is a good thing, but several things need to be in place to ensure we are not setting ourselves or anyone else up for failure:

- **Communication is key.** I can't express enough in this book, or in any talk I give, that communication is the key to genuine, authentic relationships. It is very important that we clearly communicate the objective and our expectations and, in turn, listen to what barriers may get in the way of achieving the objective. Often we have a picture in mind of what the finished product should look like, but we fail to communicate that to others. Then when our expectations are not met, we blame others. In our personal lives, it is even more profound, and can be more costly.
- **Make sure the expectations align with everyone's values.** Though this may come up while you are engaged in discussions around barriers, it may take additional questioning and going deeper. Many times our struggles are not always obvious in an initial conversation until we've had time to reflect on what is expected of us. When we start to feel conflicted, it may be because it doesn't align with our values or focus. Additional conversation needs to take place, otherwise it may happen in an unproductive, damaging, and explosive conversation.
- **Be realistic.** While stretching beyond ourselves is an excellent way to grow, we don't want to stretch so much that people snap. Be realistic about expec-

tations and setting goals. Give clear timelines and any additional assistance needed to achieve the goals.

The components above apply personally as well. How many times are we disappointed because someone did not give us what we were hoping for? I overheard Louie and his gal pal, Eve, having an interesting conversation around expectations. See if this sounds familiar:

"Happy birthday, Lou!"

"Oh thanks, Eve," he said as he looked behind her for a dog biscuit. When he didn't see anything else, he looked forlorn.

"What's wrong?" asked Eve.

"Oh nothing!" sighed Louie.

"Were you expecting something else?"

"No, of course not. You remembering my birthday is more than enough." Louie feigned a smile, and then sighed. "Well, okay, yes, I was hoping for a little more; a treat or something, you know."

"Oh, no…I didn't know. You should have said something."

"Well, if I said something, it would ruin the surprise."

"What surprise?"

"The surprise I was expecting," exclaimed Louie.

"Well, how do I know what you are expecting if you don't tell me what you're expecting?"

"Because you should just know."

Oh Louie! The harsh reality that others will not always meet our expectations is a tough lesson to learn. I suggest we not get so fixed on our expectations that we miss the possibility of far exceeding what our minds are capable of imagining. I believe it is good to dream, reach, and imagine possibilities for ourselves—just be clear on what you expect of others.

2.9

ARE YOU A SAFE LEADER— OR A SAFE PERSON, FOR THAT MATTER?

September 15th marks the anniversary of my adoption of Louie. While it seems like just yesterday he pranced into my life, many times I feel as though he has been with me for a lifetime. We both have experienced many lessons along the way.

The most important lesson has been about love—about being a loving person, not seeing others as objects, and walking out the characteristics of love: patience, kindness, and trustworthiness.

Hand in hand with love is the need for safety. I know I've shared this earlier, but a safe culture and safety in a relationship is so necessary to our well-being. Louie needed to believe I was safe. And very much like love, safety is tough to get your arms around, but I dare say everyone reading this—and those in your circle of influence—feel loved and safe.

Many times in the quietness of the night, I will hear Louie in his bed having some sort of dream, but not his usual running, playing, and jumping dream. These are disturbing, as though he is scared and he is whining. I know he is still sleeping, but I will whisper, "Lou, it's OK! Mama's here!"

He may not know what I am saying, but the very sound of my voice calms him, and he is able to relax and enjoy a good night's sleep.

<<<

MY ALPHA MOM, WHO ALWAYS MAKES ME FEEL SAFE

<<<

While taking a long stroll and Louie prances along, he will look up at me and touch his mouth to my hand. I don't profess to know what he is thinking, but I imagine it is his way of "holding hands" as we walk, just to be near and to know he is safe.

My oldest granddaughter, Evi, would be playing just a few feet from where I might have been working and rather than look up, she would call, "Nonna." I learned after a few times that she didn't want to show me anything, she didn't really want anything in particular. She just wanted to know I was near, which guaranteed her safety.

Many times I've thought of a very early childhood memory. I remember quietly walking into my parents' bedroom while everyone in the home was fast asleep. Next to my mom's side of the bed, on the wooden floor, was a little throw rug. I would lie down on the rug, just to be close to her. Often my mom would turn on her side and her hand would drop over the edge of the bed. I took that as a sign it was time for us to hold hands, so I would reach up and hold her hand. Never mind that my father was a police officer and knew how to keep a community safe. Holding my mom's hand brought immediate comfort and satisfied my

need to feel safe. I cherish the memories of holding her hand as she grew older and it was my turn to make her feel safe.

Thinking through the many times I've kept Louie safe from harm gave me pause. How safe am I as a person? A leader? A friend? A parent? How safe are you? Are you someone that, when trouble arises, others know they can approach and share from their heart without judgment or criticism or lessons? Is love your first response? Is listening with a sincere heart to really hear the other person your natural inclination? Perhaps not, but we can be intentional about how we listen. Being a safe person and providing an environment where others are able to be vulnerable and share from their heart takes discipline and wisdom. But we can all strive to be that safe person others need in times of crises and when life feels stuck.

Louie's life has been transformed because I am a safe leader. My life has been transformed because safe people surround me. Be intentional to be that safe leader, and you will see lives impacted for the greater good.

2.10 DON'T ADJUST TO YOUR DOG

How poor performance can permeate an entire team

Louie and I really enjoyed our training sessions at the Queen City Dog Training Club. Between the sessions we attended and the benefits of Zig's wisdom, we've learned a lot, but one lesson in particular stands out.

During this lesson, the instructor would have us give several commands while walking around the ring, and would observe how quickly our dogs responded. We would walk quickly and then stop; our dog would stop and sit next to us. Louie would stop and sit, but always at a 45-degree angle and while looking up at me. It looked as though he wanted to be able to see my face. Because I knew he was supposed to be right at my side, I slowly stepped closer to him until we were side by side.

"Don't adjust to your dog," came the command from our instructor, and it was directed toward me. I looked at Louie and said, "Pay attention, Lou. You're going to get us in trouble."

Once again we were told to walk around the ring and were given the command to stop and have our dogs sit next to us. Lou sat at an angle again, but this time I looked at him and then the instructor. She looked at me and said, "Don't adjust to him. Scoot his bottom toward you."

And so I did, muttering under my breath, "Why are you doing this?" He looked at me as though asking, "What did I do?"

After repeating this routine several times, I was ready to give up. Finally, Louie understood and sat perfectly still right next to me. Our training session was over but the lesson was not. The words, "Don't adjust to your dog," echoed in my mind for some time.

What was wrong with adjusting to my dog? After all, it was just one step toward him. It was hardly noticeable and in the end, we achieved what we wanted to achieve—our dogs sitting right next to us. Then it dawned on me—when I moved toward him, I was adjusting to poor performance. And I let him know that the poor performance was OK, even celebrated, if I patted him on the head.

Being flexible is very important as a leader. And we previously discussed the importance of clarity in communicating our expectations. But adjusting to poor performance is a different matter. Sometimes we adjust because we are tired of keeping the standards at the level they need to be. Many times we simply give up and take whatever we can get.

Have you ever walked into your garage and immediately noticed the pungent smell of garbage? If you stayed in the garage long enough, you would adjust to the smell and eventually no longer notice it. That is, until someone else walks in and points it out.

While not accommodating poor performance is very important for leaders, it is also true personally. So many times in society, we make adjustments in order to fit in or accept something that is wrong because we don't want to appear politically incorrect.

Recently, Evi and I listened to a radio drama about a monk named Telemachus. The story was set back in the days of the Roman Empire when the gladiator games were all the rage (long before the movie hit the big screen). Troubled by the sight of thousands assembling to see men fighting and killing one another at the Roman Coliseum, Telemachus tried to convince them that their conduct was wicked and cruel. He stood in front of thousands who were doing what was the socially accepted form of entertainment in that day and challenged them to stop such cruelty. He was immediately struck down and killed. However, his death was not in vain because after the day Telemachus was murdered in the Coliseum, no gladiator fight took place there again.

This may seem like a dramatic example compared to adjusting to a dog's slight disobedience, yet Telemachus recognized that if he didn't take action, they would continue to adjust their society to a path of moral compromise. His actions contradicted everything his society said was acceptable. People made money from the events and the gladiators were considered mighty heroes. Taking a stand cost Telemachus his life, but it changed the Roman society and, ultimately, the world.

The next time you have to make a tough choice to do the right thing, don't adjust to your "dog"—even if that dog is one cute pup looking up at you with big brown eyes saying, "Did I do good, Mom? Uh? Did I? I know I did, right?"

2.11

SUNRISE, SUNSET

Life's objective—take time to enjoy it

Louie is all boy and still very much a puppy, and sometimes that's exasperating! I try to burn off some of his energy by taking long walks, visiting dog parks, and having him run around the backyard with his buddy, Mick. But even in the middle of a nap, if Evi and Mea show up at the door, he exudes tons of energy and delivers overly excited sloppy kisses.

On one recent walk, Lou stopped to burrow his nose in the ground, hoping to find the mole he knew was near by. I waited, watched, and finally gave him a tug to resume walking, but he stubbornly refused and kept digging. Finally he jumped up, wagged his tail, and ran off to find another molehill, pulling me along. I rolled my eyes and muttered under my breath, "When is this dog going to grow up and get out of this puppy stage?"

I immediately gasped. There it was! The tendency to hurry up life. Or more specifically, my tendency to want to hurry Louie's maturity. Yet I know Lou is quickly getting older, and though it may seem like years away, he will be a senior dog before I know it. We kept walking, Louie by my side with his usual upbeat prance, bright eyes, and tongue hanging out the side of his mouth, oblivious to my thoughts of him passing through life so quickly.

Why do we try to speed up our lives? I remember cradling Marisa for her early morning feedings when she was a baby. I would look out my bedroom window as the neighborhood children waited for the school bus. Weary from sleeplessness, I thought to myself, "She will never get to that age. I will always be rocking this baby, feeding her, changing her diapers." And now I stare into the eyes of *her* children and wonder where time went. Many times while talking to my six-year-old granddaughter, if I just blink, I swear I am talking to my six-year-old daughter.

Though my father has been gone for 30 years, I have fond memories of him singing. He was a fabulous singer, although he kept his day job of being a Cincinnati Police Officer. He used to sing a song from *Fiddler on the Roof* titled "Sunrise, Sunset."

> "Is this the little girl I carried? Is this the little boy at play?
> I don't remember growing older, when did they?
> When did she get to be a beauty?
> When did he grow to be so tall?
> Wasn't it yesterday when they were small?
> Sunrise, sunset,
> Swiftly flow the days.
> Seedlings turn overnight to sunflowers,
> Blossoming even as we gaze.
> Sunrise, sunset,
> Swiftly fly the years,
> One season following another,
> Laden with happiness and tears."

<<<

ENJOYING A BEAUTIFUL SUNRISE

<<<

>>>
THE VERY FIRST PICTURE MY MOM TOOK OF ME; I WAS SCARED
>>>

As my career became increasingly more demanding, I struggled to keep my focus centered on raising Marisa. Life was at a frantic pace then and my mom would always say, "Danise, you need to stop and smell the roses." I could never understand why anyone would ever want to stop anything, much less stop to smell roses, but she was right. Life was flying by and not just mine but my child's, my family's and my friends'.

I did eventually listen to my mom and became very intentional about not rushing through life. I've learned to stop, breathe, and enjoy the moments with my daughter, family, friends, and now of course, Louie. While each stage may be but a wisp, I also believe each stage gets better because of lessons learned and deepening relationships. With each sunrise and sunset, the years swiftly fly by. One season following another, laden with happiness and tears. I enjoyed every bit of Marisa's life from the minute she was born, but the stage I am in right now with her is the best stage yet.

The month of June is usually when parents watch their children graduate, get married, or prepare for a life transition. It is also the time we reflect on where the time went. As for Louie, I cherish each crazy moment of life with him, from digging through molehills to getting excited to see his alpha pups to whining as we walk down the street because his friends, or anyone else for that matter, are out to see him. I know it will be all too soon that I will be carrying him up and down the steps as I did my former furbabies, Cece, Bree and Buffy. I know before long I will be watching my grandchildren walk the aisle to receive their diplomas. I know soon I will be saying final farewells to friends at a quicker rate than when I was younger.

For this reason, I pray you will always enjoy life to the fullest, even as you wonder where time has gone. For me, I am grateful for life and have no doubt that the best is yet to come.

2.12

PRUNING IS UNCOMFORTABLE BUT NECESSARY

The goal of removing obstacles for growth to take place

"It's that time of year, Lou," I said as I put on his leash. Louie looked at me with those big brown eyes and his brows furrowed. And then he looked at the Furminator® in my hand and started walking in the opposite direction, as though that would change my mind about dealing with his shedding. "Better outside than on my wood floor. Let's go!"

Outside we went, and I started to brush. Louie's not fond of the Furminator®, but it is a great little tool. The design of the edge allows the tool to push through the topcoat and remove the undercoat and loose hair without cutting or damaging Lou's skin. Yet no matter how gentle I am, he often tries to reach around and "deter" me.

His shedding seems particularly bad this spring. I comb him every day and still get gobs of hair. But it is a necessary practice and while I know he feels better with less hair, this form of "pruning" is not his favorite activity.

I understand that! It pains me to look at my beautiful flower garden and see the various colors popping up and bursting with life, knowing I will need to prune them back soon. I've tested the pruning method in my own garden and while it seems strange to pluck away flowers, the process gets rid of unhealthy por-

<<<

I MIGHT FEEL BETTER AFTER MY PRUNING BUT I AM NOT HAPPY

<<<

tions of the plant and allows for more robust growth. My flower garden is always beautiful mid summer, so it is well worth the pain of pruning and the patience it takes to see the results.

As Louie and I prepare for summer, we've had to take a look at pruning some things out of our lives as well. Sometimes that involves relationships that have grown stagnant or unhealthy.

By now you know my heart *and* my business are all about relationships. To be successful, one must cultivate healthy and genuine relationships. It is difficult but wise to recognize when it is time to prune relationships:

- Release people who are negative. Beware of those who continually gossip. They will drag you down and drain the energy from the relationship.
- Be a good steward of your time spent with others. There are only so many hours in a day, and we only have so much energy. Think about who brings you joy? With whom can you invest time that will result in growth? Who might you need to serve?
- Recognize one-sided relationships and let them go. While I am all about serving others, there are people who take advantage of you or your sphere of influence. Be discerning about relationships like this that may need pruning.

- Cultivate your relationship with God. In fact, start there and the difficult process of pruning other relationships can be done with grace and wisdom. You don't know what a relationship with God could even begin to look like? Ask me! That's a discussion that is well worth our time.

While it is not easy to prune relationships, it is sometimes necessary for you, and for them, to experience greater growth. Lou's shedding is winding down and he still hates the Furminator®, but he is getting better about that process.

2.13 EXPECTATIONS VS. EXPECTANCY

What's the difference?

Louie and I were walking on a beautiful fall day when we saw one of his pug buddies—or so we thought. His friend Sammy is a tan and black pug with a unique characteristic: his tongue protrudes ever so slightly. I recognized that the person walking him was not his owner. That's not unusual since many of us in the community need others to walk our dogs on occasion. Louie was excited to see his buddy and could hardly wait to romp and play.

As we approached, I asked if the dog was Sammy, because he had the same markings and the same characteristic of a slightly protruding tongue. The person walking him said no, but Louie quickly ran up to the Sammy look-alike; it did not take him long to realize this was not his buddy, and then he became indignant, as if he was mad at the pug for not being Sammy.

We quickly said our good-byes while Louie kicked up his feet and snarled, just to make sure the dog understood he was not even close to being Sammy. I realized Louie's expectations for playing with his friend were unmet, and disappointment had set in quickly. Based on all appearances, Louie was expecting to have fun and play, but that expectation was not to be filled that day.

Most people usually have a hard time moving on from unfulfilled expectations. I think these disappointments occur because we've set ourselves up for failure when we box up our expectations in the hopes that they will be fulfilled. Instead, what if we had a spirit of expectancy? You may wonder what the difference is between having expectations and having a spirit of expectancy. A spirit of

>>>
PURE JOY
>>>

expectancy is what very young children usually possess. They have the mindset that something wonderful is about to happen, but with no expectation of specifics. While they may wish for something on their Christmas list, it is their heart of expectancy that is truly magical. It is the hopefulness of something wonderful. For me, that may entail time with my family, but without expectation that the time meets any specific criteria—it is simply time together.

Expectations for particular things and events always run the risk of disappointing us, since many times, events and what others do are out of our control. Rather than focusing on the disappointments of unmet expectations, let's look forward with a heart of expectancy and see if that doesn't lighten our spirits with the hope that something wonderful is about to happen.

While Louie experienced disappointment by not having his expectations met with the look-alike Sammy, it did not dampen his spirit of expectancy. He still walks out of our home with the hope that something wonderful is about to happen. Something as simple as seeing a dear neighbor who pats him on the head or gives him belly rubs lends to his heart of wonder.

Section Three

UNDERSTANDING OTHERS

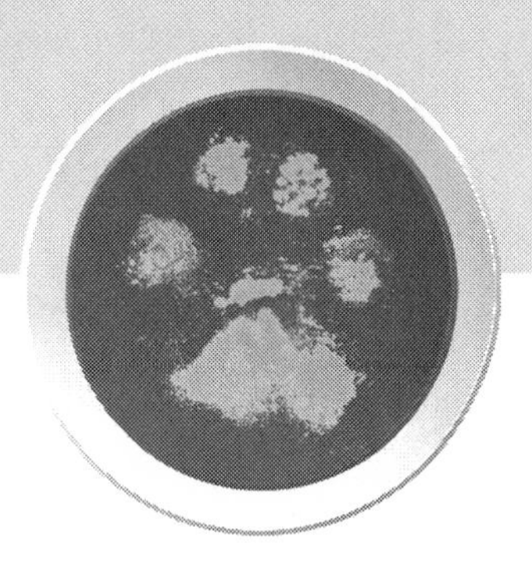

There is always one fact more in every person's case
about which we know nothing.
—Oswald Chambers

At the start of Louie's adopted life, he didn't have a very good history. He was found somewhere in Kentucky and the shelter put out an all points bulletin, but no one claimed this little dog—no one. By the time I adopted him, he had a number of issues. Fear and anxiety were at the top of the list of issues he dealt with. These may have come from abandonment or abuse—it's hard to say. Louie never had a sense of being valued in his life, and he needed to know that someone cared about him.

The next part of our journey was to truly understand Louie had "stuff" in his background. I needed to understand his issues and it wasn't easy to get past some of them. They were real and profoundly deep. I had to understand Louie's struggles in order to love him, which would enable me to set clear objectives and goals for our journey together.

This is not unlike everyone we meet, whether he or she is on our team, or a person whose path we cross in the grocery store. Every human being needs to feel loved and valued. It is our innermost need, and it was this little dog's need as well. As leaders, we need to take the time to understand our people. As Oswald Chamber's quote states: "There is always one fact more in every man's case about which we know nothing." We need to realize that there's always something about a person's circumstances that we don't know, and before we judge people, we need to try to understand them.

When you run into an issue with someone and your first inclination is to become upset and perhaps even judgmental, try the PAWS method to help you analyze the situation before doing something you may regret:

1. **P**AUSE
2. **A**SK
3. **W**ISDOM
4. **S**TOP TO SEEK AND UNDERSTAND

We've provided more detail about this process from the perspective of gossip in the chapter titled *PAWS: My What a Big Mouth You Have, Louie,* later in this section.

As leaders, we must make an effort to understand others. Take time to understand your people and avoid making assumptions. This section shares the importance of how I learned to understand Louie, who could not verbally communicate with me. These lessons will help you understand how others communicate and process ideas differently than you do—and that's OK.

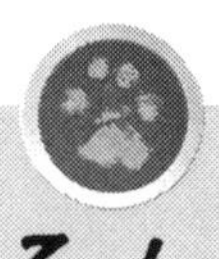

3.1

UNCLAIMED. UNLOVED. UNWAVERING.

Everyone has "stuff" in their background

Recently, I overheard my oldest granddaughter, Evi, share our dog Louie's story with her younger sister, Mea. Though you may have heard this "tail" a time or two before, I thought you would enjoy this rendition:

"A long time ago, there was a little dog who was all alone in the woods. He was scared and afraid and felt very, very alone. It was nighttime and then daylight and then nighttime, again and again. Once, he saw another little animal and thought, 'Oh, that looks like someone who could be my friend.' But the animal was a mean cat. It hissed and clawed at the poor little dog, scratching his ear till it started to bleed. 'My,' said the pup. 'I guess it doesn't want to be my friend.' The little dog still has a mark on his ear.

"The poor little dog was sad, but he kept on going because he knew somewhere, someone would love him. He was so tired that he couldn't keep his head up. He came to a road and a woman who was driving by saw him and picked him up. She took him to a place filled with lots of people and other dogs. The people called and called and called all sorts of places to find out if anyone owned the dog. They put

up signs and waited and waited, but no one came to see the little dog. He still felt all alone.

"One morning, the people put the little dog in a van and drove him far, far away. They took him to an adopt-a-pet store. There, he saw a nice lady who took him home. He was scared at first, but then the lady opened the door to her home, and two little girls were waiting for him. They hugged him and kissed his head and called him their brother. The little lost dog finally found a place he called home and two sisters who loved him very much."

Mea's mouth dropped open as she squealed, "Lou-weeeeee?"

"Yep, that's Louie's story," Evi proudly announced.

I smiled as I heard the tale so poignantly shared. Once again, Louie's story tugged at my heart as I thought about our little dog wandering the streets and wooded areas, not knowing where he was or where he should go. It is even sadder to think that despite the shelter's efforts to find his family, no one came to take him home. Louie was unclaimed and unloved—a very sad state, indeed.

Since he first came to live in my home, there has been no question that he is loved. I've gladly claimed him as my little pal, and he truly is a brother to Evi and Mea. He knows where home is. Every time we take a walk, he'll look up at me with those big, brown eyes, and I'll ask, "Do you want to go home, Lou?" With a spring in his step and dogged determination, he'll prance all the way home with little guidance from me. I have been unwavering in working through life's tough spots to build a relationship of trust, and it has paid off in huge dividends of joy for Louie and me, as well as for Evi, Mea, and many other people whom Louie has come to know and love.

Being unclaimed and unloved is not limited to adopted pups. Many people in our lives have suffered through this emotional pain. Many times these people are close friends, students, teammates, bosses, or neighbors. We never know who they are because, in today's shallow society, we don't take the time to learn about people's lives. We often wonder what is wrong with individuals who act out, but in many cases, these people may be unclaimed and unloved and are looking for others they can trust. Don't be like the cat in Louie's tale and lash out at them.

Before passing judgment on others, take the time to learn their stories. People are fascinating, and everyone has a unique history. Once you learn about someone and take the time to get to know them, you'll see them blossom and grow. Learning about others is imperative to help our team build trust and learn to walk in their strengths. Be the leader who is unwavering in working through tough spots to build a relationship of trust. This effort will pay off in huge dividends of joy and—believe it or not—productivity.

As you read this book I want you to know you are not *unclaimed* or *unloved,* no matter what has happened to you in your past. God is *unwavering* in His love for us. It is up to us to joyfully accept and receive such love.

As for Louie—he has taught me so much about love and determination and seeing past people's tough exteriors. I am never without a lesson from this little chap. He has also opened my eyes to that fact that my sweet Evi is carrying on the Nonna tradition of being the "best story maker" ever.

3.2 THERE'S NO WHINING IN DOG WALKING!

The power of vulnerability

After several months of learning leadership lessons from Louie (and his exceptional trainer, Zig), we continue to grow closer. In fact, he's my little BFF, after Evi and Mea, of course.

But I've noticed an annoying habit while we walk—he whines! Not constantly—just when we exit the garage, when we see one of his buddies (considering his excellent eyesight and keen sense of smell, that buddy could be down the street, around the bend and over the hill), or when an alpha male is in the area—and there are a lot of those around.

At first I thought he was just excited and wanted to see his friend or worse, fight his foe. But I found out from Zig that it is actually quite the contrary. He is still somewhat fearful (although he is getting better), and his whining is due to uncertainty. While I have become a very competent alpha and have provided a tremendous amount of security, Louie's still a bit skittish and not completely sure of his surroundings. He is extremely smart and learns quickly—and he remembers everything. I am sure his memory goes to a dark place when he's uncertain.

Because of this personality trait, Zig shared with me something I found fascinating. One particular day, while our dogs were playing, Louie would occasionally look over at Zig with that uncertain look, dropping his head, not really sure he wanted Zig in his space. Zig quietly proceeded to move to a sitting position on the floor, and then to a lying position. He explained that this was an extremely vulnerable position for animals, when they expose their belly. Louie, still somewhat unsure, seemed to ease up and approach Zig more easily. Zig's willingness to be vulnerable helped Louie move beyond his uncertainty and build trust.

As leaders, are we willing to be vulnerable with our teams? Are we afraid to "expose our belly," so to speak, for fear we will be seen as weak? This could be the most powerful tool in building trust within your team. And there is a delicate balance between sharing authentically and vulnerably and maintaining healthy boundaries. If a willingness to be vulnerable is not in your leadership development strategy, rethink your strategy.

Many leaders espouse appreciation for Brené Brown, author of several best-selling books on vulnerability and authenticity, but few truly walk out what she teaches. Why? Because many of us don't know how to take the first step in putting down our masks and being real. "Those who have a strong sense of love and belonging have the courage to be imperfect," she says. We are so concerned about *appearing* to be perfect; we post perfect Facebook pictures, we wear perfect clothes, our hair is perfectly coifed, and we insist others fall in line with our perfectionism, all for the sake of protecting our images. But please do not confuse excellence with perfectionism; they are completely different!

Successful organizations maintain cultures built on trust. This happens because courageous and confident leaders have a strong sense of love and belonging, and have removed their masks and aren't afraid to "expose their bellies." These leaders have a healthy balance of professionalism and transparency and enjoy truly deep, trusting relationships with their teams.

Louie whines because of doubt and uncertainty, but we have begun to build trust because I've learned from our trainer how to be vulnerable. Of course, with everything there are extremes and the key word here is *balance.* My buddy Louie seems to think that exposing his belly to me is the solution for everything. When he's done something wrong or behaves badly, I clear my throat, stand up straight, and hold one finger up in the air as I look at him. He immediately falls down to the ground and rolls over—exposing his belly. We're still working on balance.

3.3 ARE YOU A BULLY?

There's a bully in our neighborhood. For Louie (or any of us, adult or child), an encounter with a bully is unnerving and potentially devastating.

I was getting ready one morning and Louie came running into my room, almost mouthing words, mixed with a little whining as if to frantically say, "Oh my gosh, Mom, you have to come here. You have to help me because this could be really bad!"

He ran over to the window, looked out to the back yard, then looked back at me, then looked out the window again and then looked back at me, with a worried expression on his face and a lot of whining. I wondered what on earth would I see out there.

And there he was...the bully! Not just any bully—but the neighborhood's feral cat! It sauntered across the yard, causing fear and angst in Louie until it was finally out of sight. Clearly its tactics worked because of Louie's reactions.

That wasn't the only time Louie encountered his feline bully. On our walks, there's a narrow part of our path that we cross every day. One day as we came upon that spot, the bully was sunning himself and had no intentions of moving...even if approached by a hound dog with a big mouth and his human, that cat was not moving. We actually turned and walked the other way; it wasn't worth the fight.

Now I know my dog lover friends are laughing because they've seen this with their own dogs. And we've seen the funny videos of this behavior on YouTube. We also know the severity of bullying for young people and we hear more each day about the corporate bully.

Workplace bullying can include verbal, nonverbal, psychological, physical mistreatment, and humiliation. This type of hostility is particularly difficult because workplace bullies often operate within the organization's "rules" and are many times someone in authority. However, we can also be bullied by our peers, and occasionally even by a subordinate. Bullying can be covert or overt. It may be missed by superiors or known by many throughout the organization. Negative effects are not limited to the directed individuals and may lead to a decline in morale and an increase in a culture of distrust.

If you, as a leader, know there is a bully in your midst, do you resolve the issue immediately? What if no one actually complains directly about the bully, but you are discerning the rumblings and have watched enough of the body language to raise questions? Do you go to others to ask them about the person? Do you go directly to the bully to confront them, knowing you may suffer the repercussions if you express concern versus coming with actual proof you've witnessed yourself?

These are complex questions without simple answers, but the issue must be addressed…and the sooner the better.

Gossip, malicious backbiting, and passive aggressive behaviors can topple a team quickly. Rebuilding could take years, if ever. Most businesses cannot afford that type of implosion. The leader of the organization sets the tone for a culture of trust and it begins with their taking the following actions:

1. Gossip must be stopped immediately and there should be zero tolerance for it in the workplace.
2. Coworkers should be trained how to confront issues with one another in a healthy, positive manner.

As a woman in the corporate world since 1980, I have seen my share of female bullies and the unnecessary damage caused by their actions. My friend, Laurie Althaus, says it best: "They [women] attempt to mix the masculine competitive energy and individualism (which has its purpose) into the batter with the feminine strengths of cooperation, wisdom, and groupism. The two do not mix well without lots of discernment and assurance that personal values are adhered to."

While I can't do much about the neighborhood bully, as Louie's leader I can assure him that the cat will in no way interfere with his freedom to be the lovable hound dog that he is. He's learning not to react as we walk past the bully. Everyone loves to see him every day, and what a sad place our neighborhood would be if he were too scared to go on his fun walks! The same goes for your workplace. Immediately take action against bullying!

3.4
LOUIE'S AFRAID OF BIG, BLACK DOGS

Don't judge by what you think you see

Louie and I just finished our first night of obedience training and, much to my surprise, he was a superstar. In fact, the trainer took him to the middle of the arena and practiced with him as the model dog. I was shocked and wished I could have grabbed my phone to take a picture. At first, he was a little apprehensive when she took hold of his leash, but as soon as she circled him around to face me, he performed like a champ. He trotted in grand style, sat when he was told to sit, and did everything he and I practiced over the last week. I was amazed.

Something strange happened at the end of our training time. There was a very high level of energy in the facility while other groups of dogs were coming in as the previous class disbanded. Louie immediately picked up on this. He became very anxious and started a very low soft growl at the large black lab he had stood next to all night long. I immediately responded by correcting him and removed him from the ring. Crisis averted! We trotted off and headed for home.

This reminded me of something I've noticed about Louie. He seems very fearful of large black or dark brown dogs. I recognize this may be due to an aggressive stand the other dog may take toward him, but there are a few large black or chocolate labs that frighten Louie even if they are just walking with their owners.

Sometimes, if the dog locks eyes with Lou, he will take on a macho attitude and act like he's tougher than he looks.

I'm not sure where this comes from except that Louie has a very good memory. He remembers the cat from whom he took a beating; he remembers a man and cigar smoke because a neighbor walks his dogs while smoking cigars and Louie has a very strong reaction to the smell, even when the man is nowhere in sight. So some time in his past, Louie must have had a negative experience with a large black dog.

There are a couple exceptions to this fear. There is a large dark brown Doberman down the street named Rowan who is really good friends with Louie. They love to romp around with each other. Louie is so short, he fits right underneath Rowan, but apparently neither one of them have noticed. While the power of relationships is not a new phenomenon to me, I realize how important relationships are in helping dogs overcome their fears of other dogs. Much like humans, dogs remember things that frighten them or make them uncomfortable. And they will react with fear or anxiety the next time they encounter a similar situation.

When Louie first met Rowan, I sensed this might happen. However, to change that reaction, I asked Rowan's dad if Louie could check him out. He was more than happy to have Rowan sit so we could approach him very slowly and cautiously. Louie clearly sensed that Rowan was not an aggressive dog, and consequently they became friends.

This tendency to react strongly, and often unconsciously, to others is also typical of humans. Sometimes experiences have made us apprehensive of certain kinds of people—right or wrong. Unlike dogs, though, humans are easily taught not to trust or like another, and that message stays with us for a lifetime.

Unfortunately, those prejudices prevent us from building authentic relationships with people based purely on a bad experience with one person or what we have been wrongly taught over the years. Our world continues to witness the damage prejudging others has caused. And while it may seem almost too simple, being intentional about building relationships will dispel wrongful thoughts. It takes strength to not allow prejudices to control us or direct our actions and it takes courage to get out of our comfort zone.

Once Louie has an opportunity to get to know a dog of whom he might normally be frightened, he relaxes and starts to build a relationship. Now if I can just get him to drop the tough macho act, we'll be making real progress.

3.5 PRETTY LITTLE LIARS

Lying has consequences

I may sound like a broken record, but if you know me or are a follower of our leadership blog, you know how strongly I believe in authentic relationships. Humans desire deep connection with others, and dogs are no different. Trust is the foundation of a strong relationship, and without it, the relationship is weakened.

When Louie and I first met, he was so full of fear that it took months to build trust. During that time, I quickly realized that Louie had a knack for knowing truth—he's an amazing pup!

For example, he can tell where I'm going and what I'm doing simply by seeing what outfit I'm wearing. If I am dressed in a business suit and heels, he knows he is not going for a walk. If I put on my gym shoes, however, he knows his chances for a walk are greatly improved. If I combine my workout clothes and gym shoes, he waits to see if I grab the leash or head toward his cushy canine crib, which determines whether he goes with me, or must wait for me to return home.

I know Louie is not only greatly influenced by what I wear, but also by what I say and how I say it to him. If I am dressed for business and say, "I'll be right back" while sending him to his crib before I leave, he knows that in actuality I won't be right back, and he reacts to that. Saying "bye bye" to him has a different meaning as well. That means we *both* go bye bye, to the park or somewhere else for fun. When he goes into his crate and I say bye bye, this does not make sense to him. If I have my flip-flops on and start to walk out the front door and he is not in his crate, when I say, "I'll be right back," he knows I will be right back. That action usually means I am going to the mailbox. My actions and my words align. He picks up on my cues and watches my behavior just as we do when someone is sharing information with us. If their words and their behaviors do not match, we don't trust them.

I learned early in life not to lie, but this lesson particularly impacted me at age 18. I was studying to be a Radiology Technologist under the supervision of a wonderful radiologist, Dr. Howard Feigelson. He would carefully examine every set of x-ray films I took to him, diagnose what was going on with the patient, and then critique my technique. If my films were not perfect, I had an excuse for everything—the patient moved, the patient breathed, that particular machine overexposes, etc. Dr. Feigelson would sit back and look at me over the rim of his glasses and just say the nickname he coined for me, "Dani." I knew I had been busted. He was a wise man and could easily tell my words and my behavior did not line up. He then proceeded to teach me proper radiology technique as well as the dangers of habitually justifying poor performance.

As I reflected on these life lessons years later, I realized how Dr. Feigelson combined truth with love. The point wasn't only proper technique. It was the importance of being truthful and authentic. Although my parents had certainly taught me this, it was "real world" experience that made it stick. I realized I made excuses because I never wanted to disappoint him. But when I made excuses, I disappointed him even more.

This brings us back to my original point that trust is the foundation of strong relationships, which begins with being honest and truthful. We may not outright lie, but we don't exactly share the truth. Eventually, people can tell that our words don't match our actions. Consequently, trust erodes and authenticity shrinks.

Learning to **BE A**uthentic takes practice and, hopefully, this may help:

- **B**: What is the **belief** at the core of your excuse? Is it fear of exposing a mistake? Is it fear of not being liked? Is it the fear of rejection? Is it fear of inadequacy? Take time to process these questions and understand the belief.
- **E**: What **emotion** are you feeling because of the belief? Be very clear in naming that emotion and challenging it. Why is this causing such angst? Is it

worth the price you will pay in sacrificing the relationship? How will you feel if you "get by" with this excuse versus being honest?

- A: **Authenticity** is strengthened when you align your actions. To build trust, we must first align our hearts and our minds internally and then our words with our actions externally.

Louie knows that sometimes when I say, "I'll be right back" that I will not be right back, and he reacts to that. And people also sense when you make excuses, and are not being honest. It is not worth the time or energy to be anything but truthful. While we do not want to hurt others feelings, being honest is the most loving gift we can give to others!

3.6 OPEN DOORS, OPEN HEARTS

What is your open door policy?

Lou loves summer with the much-needed down time as well the extended daylight hours to play. He's had to say good-bye to a few of his sweet friends, and he's met a couple new girls on the block! There seems to be enough love in Louie's heart for all his neighborhood friends—his steady girls Ellie and Eve, and his buddies Sully, Sammy, and Mick. Now there are Jazz and Claire. He even made friends with Snickers, who originally played hard to get.

An interesting thing happened on our walks this summer. One night after a very long, hot walk, Louie hesitated when I said, "Let's go home." He knows what that means and usually prances because home is his happy place. But this time he slinked toward home. As we passed our neighbors, he looked toward their doors and garages with a forlorn expression. Finally, as we approached our home, he paused and looked up and down the street. He whined as if to say, "Can anyone come out and play?" He was like a little boy who is not ready to call it quits on a hot summer night. I sent messages to my friends and asked, "Can your dogs come out to play?" But no luck. It was time to go in, Lou!

The next day, and every day since, he has decided that every open door or garage is an invitation for him to walk right in. And off he goes to call on a neighbor. He seems particularly interested in one neighbor, June, who doesn't have a dog. Nonetheless, Lou believes her open garage door is an invitation for him to walk right in. Thank goodness June gladly welcomes Louie into her home. Other neighbors seem to love his visits as well, confirming his opinion that: "Everybody loves me!" He whines (loudly) when Claire's door is open yet she is nowhere to be found. The same is true with his other four-legged friends. My neighbors don't have to own dogs for Lou to believe he has an open invitation into their home... as long as the door is open.

I remember growing up on Cherevilla Lane where friends and family dropped in unannounced. My mom used to say, "You know who the really good friends are because they always come to the back door, knock, and then just walk in." I remember as a child actually "calling" our friends as opposed to ringing the doorbell or knocking. We would stand on the porch and melodically sing their name, "Oh Tanya." Then we would wait until someone answered the door (or yelled out that no one was home—Ha!). My friend Gina's mom told me I had the sweetest little voice when I would call, "Oh Gina!" That certainly has changed! Like Louie, if we saw an open garage door, we considered it an invitation to walk in.

Welcoming people into our offices and homes is an essential skill for leaders. I can't tell you how many times someone needed encouragement or prayer, and thankfully, my door was as open as was my heart. I've listened to coworkers and friends share about struggles, or victories, broken engagements and new jobs. We never know who is looking for an open door. It might be time to check your organization's open door policy and perhaps make a few necessary changes.

Louie believes his visits are needed and with every open door, he sees an open heart and expects a loving pat on the head. Otherwise, why would they leave their doors open, right Lou?

3.7 LOUIE AND THE INVERSE SQUARE LAW

When failure is not an option

"People process and communicate differently, is a simple message I share every chance I get. I've learned over the years to value and appreciate those differences, especially through the lessons I've learned with Louie.

I've watched him with his new gal pals as he tries to figure them out. Dakota is the shy, quiet type. Claire is the adorable, but rambunctious puppy who will soon tower over him. And Jazz is statuesque with long legs and can body slam Lou in a heartbeat—all in fun, of course. With each encounter, I watch him size up the situation and process if it is time to play or time to run away. No matter what he decides, it is comical to watch him process.

Louie and I were doing our usual stroll through the neighborhood when he started charging at something. I am keenly aware of his "danger" signals, but as I scoped the area I saw nothing to merit such a strong reaction.

Finally I saw the object of his fear. He was charging a decorative black cat. It looked like a real cat and since it didn't move even with a hound dog charging at it, it appeared to act like the cats in our neighborhood. I understood why Louie was concerned.

He walked away confused and kept looking back at the cat. He didn't understand how it could *look* real but not *be* real. All the pieces of the puzzle did not

seem to fit together. The next day he was walking with his buddy, Mick, who had the same reaction. Louie once again looked confused about a cat that wasn't real but sure looked real.

While I tried to assure Lou that it was just a fake cat, and it would not pose any danger, my words fell on deaf ears. He had to figure it out himself to fully comprehend whether it was safe or not. We could certainly draw some comparisons between people who seem authentic but aren't! But I thought of something else as I watched him—the inverse square law. I struggled with math all my life, and by comparing myself to others who seemed to catch on quickly, I thought I was stupid (even typing the word makes me cringe). Yet I actually enjoyed Radiation Physics in college—at least by the end of the course. The sequence of events that led to my entering college for Radiology and Nuclear Medicine Sciences is fodder for another chapter. Foundational to understanding radiology is a theory called the inverse square law. Without getting too technical, it is the intensity of the X-ray beam being inversely proportional to the distance from the source; the intensity of radiation becomes weaker as it spreads out from the source. Technologists must account for the distance as they set up for the X-ray. I know photographers understand this theory as well.

I had a hard time understanding this concept. Like Louie, I was confused and could not make sense of this theory—the pieces of the puzzle did not fit. My professor, the very patient and compassionate Susan Weidman, continued to work with me through a long and arduous process. Finally, I looked at her and apologized for not getting the theory. Very matter-of-factly she said, "Don't apologize to me. I am not the one who will fail the course if you don't get this theory."

It was as though the heavens parted, an angelic chorus filled the sky, and I finally saw the light—I finally understood the inverse square law. What made the difference? One little word: FAIL. Failing the course was more painful than the hard work it was going to take to figure out this theory.

While Louie is a very quick learner, there are some things that do not make sense to him. He needs time to process. Humans also need time to process. Leader, if you are a quick processor, do you show impatience with others who don't share your gift? Do you assume because you can click right through accounting formulas that others should as well? If you lead a team, does your body language show your disgust because someone can't comprehend something that seems so obvious to you?

Disdain for those who are different than we are or who learn differently will kill a team, not to mention what it does to a child. Value the differences among people, be patient, and practice servant leadership by helping others. Your team will be much more healthy and productive.

As for Lou and the black cat…he's *counting* down the days until Halloween is over.

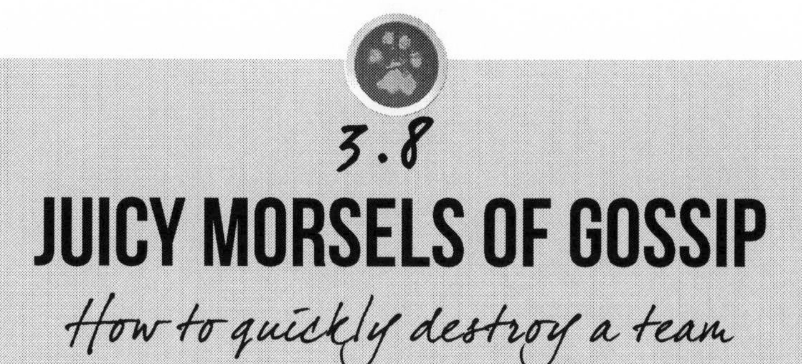

3.8 JUICY MORSELS OF GOSSIP

How to quickly destroy a team

Few of us can resist engaging in gossip. I'm not sure why, but if we reflect on our day yesterday, my guess is that many of our conversations involved tidbits of information about others (all justified, of course). Perhaps all of us could learn a few tips from Louie on this subject.

Louie and I were taking our usual early morning walk and the sun had not quite risen. As we were rounding a bend we heard voices, which gradually escalated. I continued walking as we passed a couple who were in the middle of a disagreement while walking toward their respective cars. Louie's ears perked up as he gave an alert signal—or more of a "Danger, Will Robinson! Danger!" signal. He wanted nothing to do with this couple and took off in the opposite direction.

I, on the other hand, lingered for a few minutes and pulled him back, hoping he would take a potty break. Why? Because I wanted to listen in! I didn't even know this couple, but I wanted to peek into their world long enough to learn all about this conflict. But Louie was determined to get as far away as possible…so I turned and headed in the direction he wanted to go—away from the arguing couple. Louie's (and most humans') aversion to conflict is future material. This was different. This was not *my* conflict that I needed to deal with but rather someone else's conflict, which I wanted to enter into from a safe distance as a fly on the wall. As you read this, you are probably agreeing with me that you do the same thing. Why is that?

There is something in human nature that can't resist throwing ourselves into someone else's drama. And with limited information, we decide to share what little we know about the situation with others, mainly to make us feel good about ourselves. After all, *we* aren't arguing with someone as we walk to the car—so there must be something wrong with *those people*, not with us, right?

But when we display this behavior at work, it destroys a team. And when a leader is the one who instigates gossip, they cultivate an unhealthy, distrustful culture. An article in *Harvard Business Review* stated, "Gossip is not a problem; it's a symptom. The symptom disappears when a critical mass of leaders stop enabling it, create trust in healthy communication channels, and invest in building employees' skills to use them." I know that to establish a "no-gossip zone," leaders must:

- Model a no-gossip policy in their own lives.
- Not engage in others' drama.
- Refuse to listen to others when they start to gossip.
- Step back and ask themselves, "What is going on with me that I feel the need to share this information?"

These are just a few no-gossip strategies, but they offer a good place to check our own behavior. Louie had the right idea: turn and walk the other way. Don't

<<<
MY PROM DATE, DAKOTA
<<<

get involved in other's business unless invited for counsel. Use your words to build up and affirm people; be careful about what you say. I believe this proverb says it best: "The words of a gossip are like choice morsels; they go down to the inmost parts."

Whether you are a leader or teammate, if you have even a slight inkling you should *not* share something about another person—STOP! Don't do it! Turn and walk away. Establish a no-gossip zone for your entire organization, and you'll see a difference in your organizational culture.

3.9 ADDRESSING CONFLICT

By now you know that Louie has a few issues. He sometimes acts tough when actually he is afraid, he doesn't like anyone coming into our house, and he absolutely does not like conflict.

You might wonder how a dog can know anything about conflict. Well, his actions speak volumes. He runs from any type of confrontation the minute it begins. Clearly, this type of behavior doesn't work in the "real" world of business. Interestingly, a healthy culture that promotes trust requires dealing with conflict.

So we decided to talk to one of Louie's gal pals, Ellie Ruhl, whose mom is an expert on dealing with conflict. Here's what we learned:

LOUIE: Ellie, I was wondering if you could help me. My Master Mom seems to think I have an aversion to conflict. Since your Master Mom, Lynne Ruhl, is an expert on healthy cultures and helps people all over the world deal with conflict, perhaps you can give me some advice?

ELLIE: Of course, Louie. I'll certainly try. Tell me why your Mom thinks you have this aversion.

LOUIE: Uhh, well, I run every time there's conflict. It's very uncomfortable! There's growling, baring of teeth, loud voices all around. Makes my stomach hurt just thinking about it.

ELLIE: Louie, that does sound uncomfortable. Does it frighten you?

LOUIE: No, not at all.

(ELLIE tilts her head and continues to look at Louie with her adorable big eyes.)

LOUIE: Well, maybe just a little.

ELLIE: That's understandable. After all, just from the body language alone, there is a clear message being sent, right? In our culture, when a dog bares his teeth he is sending you a clear message to back off or else.

LOUIE: Right, and I get that message loud and clear and take off running. Don't have to tell me twice.

ELLIE: That's probably the best approach when you're dealing with a fellow canine. But when dealing with humans, sometimes the best approach is to take some time to process what's going on and then deal with the issue. You're not alone. Most people don't know how to deal with conflict. It really is uncomfortable. But the alternative is living with suppressed anger or resentment, which eventually leaks out, causing harm to us and others. So it is best to deal with it.

LOUIE: I know Ellie, you're right. You're always right. So show me some steps I should take to deal with conflict more effectively.

ELLIE: Sure, Louie. I'd be happy to.

- First, take time to cool down. Step back and assess what's going on inside you.
- Seek to understand what the other person might be experiencing.
- Pay close attention and let them share whatever is going on for them. See things from their perspective. And most importantly, listen.
- When you seek to understand the other person's position, your body language and attitude will soften and won't look "scary" to them.

LOUIE: Ok, thanks El. And this works?

ELLIE: Oh yes, it works for my Mom every time. Remember, dealing with conflict can be uncomfortable, but losing a friend is heartbreaking.

LOUIE: Wow, Ellie, that makes so much sense. This has been really helpful. I wonder if my Master Mom knows this information.

ELLIE: Oh, of course she does Louie. She uses it all the time.

LOUIE: Thanks, Ellie. I think I will do better next time I'm around conflict. You're a great friend to help me out with this.

ELLIE: You're welcome, Louie. I appreciate our friendship. And you know I really love your Mom, right?

LOUIE: Of course, [sniff], I know that [gulp]. I'm good with that, El.

3.10

BRAVADO OFTEN MASKS FEAR AND PRIDE

Look beyond the tough exterior

If you've read our blog or this book from the beginning, you know the issues I've had with Louie, and how fearful he can be. I've learned many valuable lessons from our trainer, Zig, but one in particular continues to make an impact on us. Zig shared that Louie puts on an act of bravado by growling and barking because he's masking how fearful he actually is. "You don't want him to act out in fear because that can be very dangerous," said Zig. "You can never be sure what a fearful dog might do."

I recently reflected on this wisdom Zig offered some time ago. After an intense amount of work on building Louie's trust in me and in others, his fear has all but subsided (except for a chance confrontation with a cat or someone new at my door). Occasionally I see a fearful reaction arise and in a second, if he can't run (which is his first choice), he turns into a fierce dog. But just as quickly, with one command from me, he leaves it and moves on.

What is it about fear that causes such strong reactions? Sometimes we are afraid of something and, in a second, we make a rash decision to lash out or run. Sometimes sheer determination can look like courage when, in reality, we are aggressively masking our fear.

Police officers, firefighters, and other emergency personnel know what it's like to make split-second decisions that override their fears. Their training has prepared them to act in the best interests of others—despite how they feel inside —because lives are at stake.

But what about the times when fear drives us to make a split second decision that is not in the best interests of us or others? Many times fear and pride go hand in hand and it becomes a vicious cycle. Fear of losing jobs, relationships, social status, leadership, or influence can drive us to make ourselves look better on the outside and attempt to make others smaller by comparison.

I thought about this crazy cycle as I watched the Bengals' loss of the playoff game. Was it the fumble or the two plays at the end, or the penalty flags thrown? Or was it the vicious cycle of fear and pride?

I'm not a football strategist and talking football is a far stretch from dealing with little Louie and his fears, but everyone in leadership can learn lessons about dealing with fear and pride. Fear itself isn't necessarily wrong—it's a sign that we could be in danger and need to take the necessary physical or emotional precautions. And certainly we can take pride in a job well done. But when fear is unfounded and pride is rooted in self-centeredness, the perfect storm develops and the vicious cycle begins. Sadly, the consequences can have an ongoing ripple effect, as we witnessed during the playoff game.

We need to choose our mode of operation *before* we find ourselves in situations where we might become fearful and reactionary. Firefighters and police officers are well trained prior to facing the dangers of their jobs. We would all do well to spend a little time assessing our fears, examining the issues that could cause us to operate out of self-centered pride, and identifying steps we can take to eliminate a knee-jerk reaction. Though I still have a long way to go, I've learned to stop for a moment before responding because that brief moment might prevent a negative reaction I may later regret. A "Help me, Lord," is never a bad idea either!

As for Louie, I think he acts tough not only out of fear, but also out of his love for and desire to protect me. He has learned to control it because when I give a command, he listens. Somewhere behind those big brown eyes, he knows I love him and will always protect him.

3.11

PAWS: MY WHAT A BIG MOUTH YOU HAVE, LOUIE

The power of the tongue

We were enjoying an early morning walk when we came upon two dogs we've never met before. One of them was a twin of Louie. She was a Corgi-Beagle mix, and she even had the same facial markings as Louie. She was a bit smaller than Louie, and her owner called her Peanut.

There was a noticeable difference, however, in the size of their mouths. Like her name, she was a peanut, and her mouth was tiny compared to Louie's very big mouth. Louie's mouth can do many things: bark, growl, show his teeth, eat, and mouth to pull and play. Louie provides "love taps" by poking his mouth against your hand when he is excited to see you. His mouth is conveniently attached to his nose, which he uses to poke and prod. They work together to borough in the ground and pull lumps of grass to get to a mole.

Although Louie's large mouth is actually harmless, he could do a lot of damage with it. This is not unlike ourselves. Our mouths, specifically our tongues, may seem harmless, but oh the damage they can do and usually, unnecessarily.

I love what the Bible teaches us about the tongue. "A bit in the mouth of a horse controls the whole horse. A small rudder on a huge ship in the hands of a skilled captain sets a course in the face of the strongest winds. A word out of your mouth may seem of no account, but it can accomplish nearly anything—or destroy it! It only takes a spark, remember, to set off a forest fire. A careless or wrongly placed word out of your mouth can do that. By our speech we can ruin the world, turn harmony to chaos, throw mud on a reputation, send the whole world up in smoke and go up in smoke with it..." and "You can tame a tiger, but you can't tame a tongue—it's never been done." (James 3: 3–7)

We have the power to use our words to give life or to bring death to our relationships. Hurtful words can be used in slander, gossip, arguing, criticizing, complaining, distasteful language, boasting, and lying. And the damage can be irreparable. As we read that list, we shake our heads for we clearly know others who do these things. Yet, there's a small voice within us that whispers, "Could this be me?"

I believe we are all guilty of some or all of these things. For the sake of brevity, let's focus on the first two: gossip and slander. By definition, gossip is sharing personal or sensational facts about others; sharing private information with those who are not part of the problem or solution. Slander is using words, tonal patterns, or facial expressions to deliberately damage someone else's reputation with information that does not need to be shared.

We all do this either subtly or with as much gusto as possible, and perhaps we are not aware of the damage we are doing. I am most grieved by those who teach and preach against gossip and yet do so under the guise of caring for the person they are talking about, or worse, having the need to play the victim role and share how unfair, someone treated them.

It takes intentionality to not step foot on the slippery slope of gossip and slander. It is not easy, but commit to using the PAWS method once again to help before doing something you may regret (like getting into a gossip session).

Through my relationship with Louie, I have learned a tremendous amount about my relationships with humans. With the size of his mouth, he could take a chunk out of someone, but he clearly chooses not to. In that same way, I want nothing to stand in my way with those who are in my life, even those with whom I interact for a short time. I am going to stamp out gossip and slander in my life using the PAWS method. I hope you will join me.

PAWS

1. **P**AUSE: Breathe! Allow oxygen to get to your brain. There is power in the pause. When we pause before speaking, we gain time to process our thoughts. I'd rather make people uncomfortable with my pause than with my words. I've never regretted my pauses, but too many times, I have regretted my words.
2. **A**SK: Ask questions, and in this case of gossiping, ask yourself these things: What's going on with me? Why do I have this need to share this? Would I want this person sharing information about me? Would I share this if the other person were in front of me? Reflect on your answers before you speak.
3. **W**ISDOM: Choose your words wisely. When we speak from a place of wisdom, people are more inclined to listen. Carefully consider the words you are about to say. If they are not life giving, do not say them. Nothing good comes from useless, mindless words.
4. **S**TOP AND SEEK TO UNDERSTAND: Stop gossiping for one day and truly seek to understand others. When we want to lose weight, we log our food to keep track of what we are putting into our bodies. Take a day this week to log how many times you talk about someone else. That may make you more aware of how easily gossip has seeped into your life. Then ask a friend to hold you accountable when you are together, and commit to not talking about others.

3.12 LOUIE, YOUR REPUTATION PRECEDES YOU

Louie has this funny little habit of whining when he sees his pals. You can hear him all the way down the street. People will turn and wait as Louie's whines get louder and his tail wags faster. He'll run towards the person or one of his furry friends. He excitedly greets them and then BOOM! He's on to the next friend.

People know he's going to do that to them. They watch him run and hear his excitement and after a few doggie sniffs he quickly moves on. My neighbors fully expect him to behave this way because they've witnessed this so many times. And now it's the talk of the neighborhood…how snooty little Louie DiStasi can be.

I make excuses and justify his behavior by saying things like, "He's very focused on his walk," or "Don't take it personally, he's anxious to keep moving." It is obvious his reputation clearly precedes him as we walk through the neighborhood.

This behavior had me ponder the importance of our reputations. It is much harder to build a reputation than to destroy it. Building a good reputation requires patience, solid values, intentionality and time. Destroying a good reputation only requires a single moment's mistake. To build a good reputation, be a person who is worthy of one. Demonstrate the characteristics you want others to associate with you.

I had the honor and pleasure to work with Ken Blanchard in early 2000. During a workshop in 2001, Ken shared a memorable exercise that left an indelible imprint on my mind and heart.

Ken told a story about Swedish chemist, Alfred Bernhard Nobel, who invented dynamite in 1866 and became rich. Nobel was as interested in drama and poetry as he was in chemistry and physics, but it was in the sciences that he made his fame, and by the time of his death he held more than 350 patents and controlled factories and labs in 20 countries.

When Alfred Nobel's brother died, a newspaper mistakenly published an obituary of Alfred that emphasized the fact that he had invented things that blew up and killed people. Nobel, not wanting to be remembered in that way, pledged his wealth toward the betterment of humanity. In his will he directed the establishment of a foundation to award annual prizes for achievement in chemistry, physics, literature, and efforts toward international peace, which is known as the Nobel Prize. This award is considered one of the most prestigious awards in the world and includes a cash prize of nearly one million dollars.

Ken asked, "What do you want your obituary to say about you?" He had the participants write out their thoughts. And then he asked, "What do you have to do today to be the person you want to be remembered as?"

That exercise had a profound effect on me then, and still does today. I don't want to be gone and people have to drum up something about me being a compassionate and deeply caring person. I commit to living out those characteristics today.

I encourage you to do the exercise Ken has had so many people around the world engage in doing: write your own obituary. Take time to figure out how you want to be remembered and then commit to being that person today!

As for Louie, it may be too late. It seems his reputation precedes him and not in a good way. We'll have to continue to work on his relational skills and how he engages with others. Stay tuned!

3.13
WALKING SIDE BY SIDE
A process for conflict resolution

It seems that disrespect for people with differing opinions is at an all-time high in our society today.

The rude rhetoric on all sides of the political spectrum during the 2016 elections gave me pause and made me think of Louie and some of his not-so-friendly foes. I am convinced that if people were to act the way our pets do, we would all get along better. For example, sometimes Louie might see a dog that challenges him. The two will snarl and growl and perhaps even bark at each other. However, the minute we walk side by side with the dog and its owner, they seem to get along. There is something about being intentional and walking alongside someone you have a disagreement with.

Louie has done this with my niece's dog, Buddy. Those two little boys will scrunch their noses, curl their lips, show their teeth, stand their hair up, and bark in such a high pitch that people turn their heads with a look of concern. Andrea laughs, assuring everyone in sight that the dogs are actually cousins and are fine with each other. It sure doesn't seem like it when they are facing one another. However, as soon as we start walking, they are fine together.

Louie also behaves this way with rambunctious Claire, his other cousin Noli, his neighbor Snickers, and a new boxer in the community named Socks. What is it about being side by side with their supposed nemesis? I think there are several things:

1. It is less threatening.
2. They are on equal ground.
3. They see the same vision of what lies ahead.
4. They walk with the same pace.
5. It is easier to carry the other's burden. (Okay, this one relates to humans, not Louie.)

What if some of our leaders were intentional about walking side by side instead of duking it out? I am reminded of an article I wrote in 2005 with Ken Blanchard titled, "Leading with Your Heart Takes Humility." Although it was written several years ago, the premise holds true today: *Humility is the key to excelling in leadership.* And servant leaders are humble enough to walk beside someone they disagree with.

I won't share the full article, but here are some of the highlights:

1. Something is glaringly missing from leadership today. Sadly, many leadership programs are missing just one key ingredient: the heart. Not just the heart of the issue or the heart of the matter—the heart of the people.
2. What gets in your way? What truly is your motive for being a leader or wanting to lead others? Is it for selfish gain or to better others?

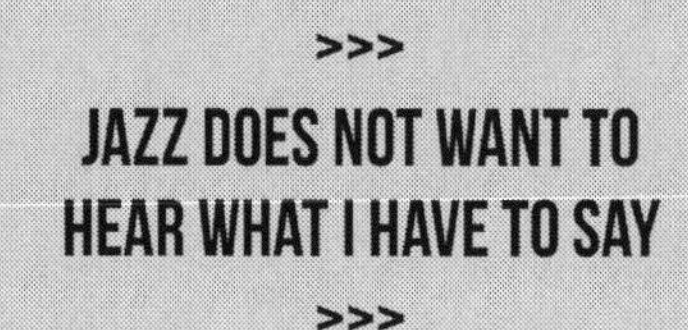

<<<
SIDE BY SIDE WITH MY FLUFFY FRIEND
<<<

3. Many times, our ego gets in the way and what bubbles up out of our hearts are things like pride, selfishness, and even fear.
4. How can you push past what holds you back? In getting past the barriers, is the challenge as a leader to balance confidence with humility to fight ego issues? Every time you make a leadership decision, are you thinking of yourself or others?
5. Confidence does not come from being in a dominant position and leading by intimidation. Doing this will cause you to lose respect from others, and any talk about values or integrity will be ignored. Humility, however, is not something they teach us in business schools. It is a character trait that is honed over time with truth and love.

Our schools, businesses, organizations, and families are hungry for leadership coupled with humility. It takes commitment to make the necessary changes to have a healthy culture and humble leaders.

Perhaps our world could learn a lesson from Louie about being intentional and walking side by side with others rather than snarling at them. While Louie doesn't understand humility, his actions speak louder than his woof. He is more than willing to walk alongside others. As I watch his actions, I am convinced that we humans have much to learn from our dogs.

3.14

LOCK EYES WITH PEOPLE—THEY MATTER

Louie is one smart dog. I know most dog owners say that about their dog, but truly…this little guy is amazing.

For instance, we'll be taking a long walk, and typically Louie can walk quite a distance. But sometimes, if he's been on a long run with his friend and walker, Mary, he'll let me know he's tired. He'll slow down, lower his head, and look straight into my eyes as if to say, "Can we slow it down a bit?"

I'll ask him if he wants to go home and he'll spin right around and trot back toward our home, with a sudden burst of newfound energy.

He does this quite a bit, but what gives me pause as I reflect on this interchange is how Louie locks eyes with me. He doesn't just look at me, he actually locks eyes with me and then seemingly communicates his message. He does this often. Not a word passes between us, not a hand signal, not a sound, and yet he understands me and I understand him. Now that is an amazing dog.

Other times as we walk he'll just reach up with his mouth to touch my hand. I'll look at him and again, he'll lock eyes as if to say, "I just wanted you to know I'm still here."

Then I started to take note of how often Louie locks eyes, not only with me, but with others as well:

- When he comes across a dog that he is unfamiliar with, he will stare, lock eyes, and possibly challenge.

- When someone comes into my home, he will stare, lock eyes, and definitely challenge them.
- When I am in the kitchen cooking, he will stare, hoping to lock eyes with me so that I will fall into his trance and hear him say, "Give me a piece of the food you are preparing that smells so wonderful. That's right, just drop it on the floor, and I will love you forever."
- He locks eyes with me during my quiet time with God in the mornings and seems to sense a peace and calm. I'll look over at him on his bed, and we'll lock eyes as if to say, "All is well!"
- He locks eyes with Mea and Evi when they give belly rubs.
- And he locks eyes with the drivers in big black trucks that he mistakenly believes is my son-in-law delivering Mea and Evi to my home

I could go on because he has this very uncanny way of locking eyes and communicating a message that takes no words.

My mom and dad always taught me to lock eyes with people because they matter. That resonated with me then and still does today.

Leaders who have honed their relational skills and are extremely effective and successful have practiced the small and seemingly insignificant behaviors that let others know they are valued and loved. In our very superficial world where most of the people we pass have their faces plastered against their phones, take a few minutes to truly lock eyes with someone and let them know they matter. You can significantly shift a person's world for the better.

Louie loves to communicate with his eyes and so far, I am the blessed recipient of his "lock and load 'em up with love" big brown eyes! Yep, I feel loved!

3.15

THE REMNANTS OF A BAD BEHAVIOR

My granddaughter always corrects me when I say Louie is a bad dog. She says he is not a bad dog; he just has a few bad behaviors.

OK, I understand the change in wording. But honestly, Louie can make my life somewhat difficult.

Louie is a superstar when we walk around the neighborhood, when I take him to visit clients, or when he accompanies me to speeches and workshops. And those of you who have had him visit your business will be shocked by what I am about to say.

Louie still reacts strongly when people come into my home. Even though he is only 40 pounds, he is all muscle, and he has a huge mouth. His bark is very deep, and his growl is deeper, and he acts like he wants to kill you. Let's be clear: Louie does not want you in my house. Don't bring a dog into my house or even onto my driveway, because the hackles go up and the teeth come out.

Yes, I am describing Louie, the same dog many of you believe is so sweet, the one with big brown eyes and an adorable face.

Now I know Louie well enough to know he's not being mean but has some misguided notions that I need protection from friends of mine who come to visit. I appreciate that, but it can be quite a hassle to make him settle when I have company. And it would not be helpful to let his bad behavior continue and just ignore him.

Those friends brave enough to risk Louie's wrath have learned to allow the time and needed discipline, knowing eventually he will settle down.

His bad behavior was front and center recently when my sister-in-law came to Cincinnati for a reunion and stayed with us in our home. She came in Friday evening, texted me to let me know she had arrived, then knocked softly on the door. Complete mayhem broke out. I kept Louie in the kitchen behind a gate and paid little to no attention to him while we said our hellos. I did my usual routine of discipline and he settled pretty quickly. Then we let him join us. He sat right at my feet as Agnes and I visited, but the minute she moved, the loud barking began, and he tried to make her stay in her place. He must have some basset hound in him because his bark is so deep. His Corgi side tries to herd everyone in my house. And the beagle side? Well, let's just say thank goodness for that silly funny beagle side of him.

By the next morning, he was sitting by her door, waiting patiently for her to come out. They had become fast friends, and by the time she left on Monday, he was very sad to see her go. I reflected on their relationship as compared to a human relationship.

Most people would write off Louie as a nuisance or would be fearful of him. They wouldn't give him much hope of ever developing a relationship because, well, he's just a bit abrasive. And when he startles my company with a very quick reaction to them, he is stepping out of line, and who needs that?

But Agnes persevered and overlooked Louie's many quirky behaviors. She talked sweetly to him, and his low growls and loud basset barks subsided. The rest of my family has learned to love on him as well, making it a bit easier to have an Italian family who loves to get together—crazy dog and all.

How many people do we write off as a nuisance or are we fearful of because of their "bark"? Many times people may have a quirky behavior that's different than what we're used to, and yet, given time and love, they may be as warm and loving as Louie under his tough bravado act.

Is it easy to love people who seem unlovable at first? No, of course not. It's hard to love them and it takes time. But if someone is in your life, they have come across your path for a reason. Don't waste time judging their quirkiness. Loving others is not an option; it is why you are on this earth.

Now that Louie and Ag are BFFs, maybe he'll be nicer to people coming into my home. I won't count on it, though!

3.16

SOMETIMES WE HAVE TO WALK WITH A LIMP

Understanding humility

Louie and I have been making our rounds, speaking to various groups and visiting businesses and organizations. He is, indeed, a transformed dog, and loves the accolades he receives as we share the story of our journey together.

A few weeks back, my granddaughter, Evi, noticed a growth on Louie's right rear paw. We took him to King's Veterinary Hospital to visit Dr. Paul LaCompte. He promptly diagnosed the wart on Louie's paw pad as a possible sign of the papillomavirus and told us to watch it for a couple of weeks. It looked like it would have naturally fallen off, except that the nail on an adjacent toe seemed to increasingly irritate the possible wart.

One Sunday, I noticed the condition seemed to be worsening, so I bandaged it and hoped Louie would be okay until we could get in to see Dr. Paul the following day. As we took a short walk, we stopped to chat with a neighbor and, genuinely concerned for Louie, she asked about the bandage. I explained what was going on and said that we would try to see the vet the next day.

She leaned over, petted Lou, and said, sweetly but with a sad face, "Awww, Louie. I'm so sorry. You're not that perfect little boy now." I responded, "And he's thinking, 'You would never know I was not perfect if my mom hadn't put on this stinkin' bandage.'" We laughed, and Louie and I continued with our walk.

Dr. Paul and his team did see Louie that Monday and suggested surgery that day. They promptly removed the growth and sent it off for a pathology report. As usual, they did a fantastic job; they doted on him, stitched him up, and instructed me on his care for the next couple of weeks. He walked a little slower, but was happy to go home that same evening.

When we arrived home, I took Louie out for a short stroll. As we walked, I watched him limp a bit, then pick up his stitched leg to run on three legs, and then, every so often, do a skip. Reflecting on the comment my neighbor had made, I realized that neither Louie nor I would ever claim he is perfect. But as I watched him walk with a limp, this thought gave me "paws."

I wondered why we often work so hard to give the appearance of being perfect. Maybe we try hard not to appear "so perfect," but we certainly don't let others see us with our masks off, do we? And while people do not need to know every single thing that we think is wrong with us or that we try to hide from others, the key to dropping our masks and being genuine and authentic is humility! Every humble, successful, and effective leader I know "walks with a limp."

British author and scholar C. S. Lewis wrote: "Humility is not thinking less of yourself. It is thinking of yourself less." I struggled with this issue for many years. I wanted people to see that I had it all together and was pretty darn near perfect. That could not have been further from the truth. In fact, hiding behind that perfect mask was a lie! I wasn't a perfectionist by any stretch of the imagination, but I sure did not want people to see the real me because I didn't want anyone to have a reason not to like me.

Am I the only person who has ever struggled with this? I don't think so. But the cost of wearing a mask kept me from being real and authentic, and hindered my use of the God-given talents and gifts I've been blessed with. I've learned to be okay with walking with a limp, in more ways than one.

The pathology report came back with good news; the growth was just what Dr. Paul thought—a papilloma. Louie and I took a nice walk to celebrate. As I watched him, I appreciated the little lesson he had passed on to me. He doesn't care what anyone thinks if he limps. If he can get out and has to walk with a limp, by golly, he's going to go out and walk with a limp. Walking outside with his mama is much more important than trying to appear as if he has it all together, even if it means walking with a limp.

And so it should be with us. Removing all the pretenses of perfection is freeing. So what if you happen to limp a bit? How are you doing with letting down the mask and letting people see your flaws? It may be worth it to take some time to PAWS and reflect on this!

Section Four

INVEST IN OTHERS

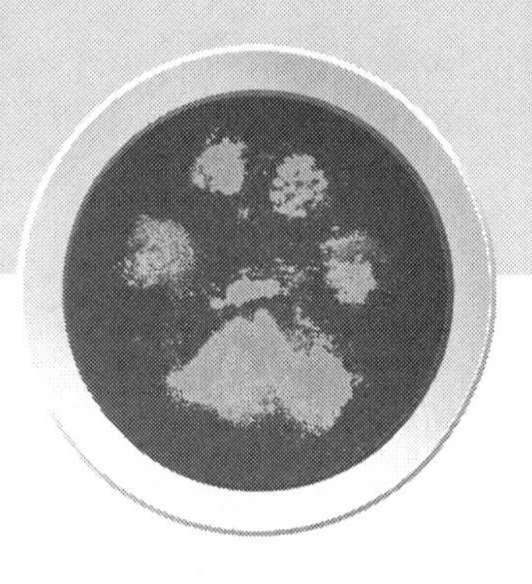

"One of the greatest values of mentors is the ability to see ahead what others cannot see and to help them navigate a course to their destination."

—John C. Maxwell

This is a sketch that my granddaughter, Evi, did of Louie the first night he came home to live with me. He curled up in the corner, scared and alone. I put a pillow next to him to provide some comfort. It was at this very moment I decided to invest what I could to help this little abandoned pup to feel worth and value and to know he was loved.

The next part of my journey involved investing my time and talent into developing Louie. I chose to invest a tremendous amount of time in Louie so that he could learn to trust and love me. It took time. Everything takes time. You cannot go wrong by investing your time getting to know people. Take them out to lunch. Ask them questions. This point relates back to understanding. It links to feeling valued, and it relates to feeling loved. Take time to gather information. You never know what you can uncover when you give your time.

There are many suggestions for, and examples of, investing in others throughout this section. Get to know people, spend time with them, and share your talents and your skill set; put effort into your relationships with people because you want to give without receiving anything in return. I can guarantee that if you are a leader, and you do this, your team will be more productive, creative, and effective. It is the foundation for a healthy culture. Invest your time.

4.1

ARE YOU POURING INTO OTHERS?

Louie and I have been together for a number of years. I realize we've learned so much from each other, but that doesn't mean I've forgotten how tough it was in the beginning.

Louie went from lock down at 8:30 p.m. in a cushiony, penned area in my bedroom to a fluffy royal bed, completely opened. He goes to bed on his own (still at 8:30 p.m.) and even if he wakes up before I do, he patiently waits for me to give the command, "Here." Only then does he move off his bed.

While I have always been an early riser, it was an adjustment for me to get up, get dressed and get outside between 5:30 and 6:00 a.m. Now we do it every single morning, regardless of weather. And believe me, it's not been easy with some of the winters we've had in the Midwest!

He patiently sits as I fill up his food bowl and doesn't move until I nod my head and say, "Go." He walks by my side and rarely pulls and immediately sits prior to our walking across a busy street until I give the "Go" command. We're still working on how he greets guests, but overall he has improved immensely.

So why such great improvement? Because I've poured energy into him; not for a few weeks—but for years. And I will continue to pour into him. I didn't have to give him so much time and love. He probably would have been an average dog without any training or time. But I chose to pour into him with no real "return on investment" and certainly no guarantee that he would be worth my time.

These last few years have brought out the best in Louie. His trainer poured into us and now Louie's true character and behavior have been given an opportunity to develop. No doubt, he is a much happier pup.

The significance of pouring energy into others is equally important for leaders. We can't expect to hand over a manual, put the new team members through orientation, and check in with them occasionally. It takes consistent time and energy to bring out the best in people.

I am thankful for those along my journey who have poured into me. They didn't need to, they *chose* to with no guarantees that it would work. I know many leaders who "mentor" others, but there is always some sort of return for them. Rarely is it to make a difference in that person's life—they are too busy for that.

I've had two mentors who made a difference in my life. I would not be the woman I am today without their love, time, wisdom, and accountability. They had nothing to gain by spending so much time with me, yet they did. Kathryn Rose Norman walked with me on my spiritual journey when no one else was willing. (I was a lot like Louie; a little rough around the edges.) She introduced me to Lynne Ruhl, who also poured into me for more than a decade and continues to do so. Thank you seems so insignificant for what they did for me. I'm a lot like Louie in that I will seek to demonstrate my gratitude for a long time to come!

Their investment in me has inspired me to invest in others. I rarely refuse to spend time with those who may need some guidance or encouragement, although

I have nothing obvious to gain. I maintain healthy boundaries, but I always welcome an opportunity to invest in another's life. Though I may not see an earthly "return," in God's economy, I am always richly blessed!

Now if I can just get Louie to stop using his big mouth (literally) when he plays and roughhouses! While I'm glad he's playing, it's clear we have more work to do—and that's just fine by me.

4.2 WHEN THE WORLD WAS SILENT

Take time to truly know people

It is early Saturday morning, after a fun Halloween night, and it already looks like a blustery, cold weekend. As I'm writing, one "like" after another pops up on my Facebook page, and my attention is continually diverted to review the latest comment. My daughter posted a picture of my adorable grandchildren dressed up for Halloween. Nonna had to get in on the fun and dressed up as Cruella De Vil—no costume needed, just a brush of the hair to expose the white streak that has been invading my dark head of hair over the last few years. It worked, and the "likes" were popping up by the second.

Louie, however, was unimpressed. As he sat in his favorite chair and sighed, he looked at me with those big brown eyes. "Mom, remember when the world was silent?"

"Hmmm," not wanting to be distracted from my computer, "No, Lou, I don't remember any such thing."

"Well, I sure do." He sighed, deeper this time. "Long, long ago when you picked up your new phone and it wasn't working quite right, you had to go without it for a day, remember?"

I continued typing, "It was actually just three weeks ago and it wasn't working at all!" I stopped typing and looked at him. I grimaced as I thought back on that time. If there is ever an area where my patience is tested, it is in the area of technology. I consider myself very proficient in understanding technology, an understanding that dates back to my college days of learning the intricate, technical design of radiology and nuclear medicine diagnostic imaging equipment. I expect technology to work well, but it will never work fast enough for me, no matter how advanced it becomes. When I picked up my new phone, it had several issues, and I could not return to the store until the next day. So I had to do without it for a day.

"I remember we took long walks together, we talked, and you actually looked at me when you talked to me," Louie observed.

"Lou, aren't you being a little dramatic? I take you on long walks now, right?" DING, another "like," and I'm right back on my computer, laughing out loud at the latest snide comment on the post.

He leaned back in the chair and sighed as he longingly looked out the window. "I rest my case!"

"Awww, Lou, come on! It's not that bad," I said, not looking up. "I know I'm on my computer a lot, but I'm a writer and that means computer time."

He then sat straight up and looked at me with an intense, soul-searching look. "It's not about the computer, Mom, or the likes or the funny comments."

I closed my computer and sat for a minute looking at my pup. After staring intently at one another, I suddenly understood the message his body language and facial expressions were trying to relay to me. Yes, Louie, I remember when I didn't have my phone for a day and it seemed the world was silent and it was wonderful. That time of disconnection was a welcome reprieve from the bombardment of social media.

Today, people will write just about anything in their posts, articles, and advertisements. Truth seems to be a commodity that is regarded as silly, or worse, not necessary. A business can tout how healthy their culture is, yet the only person giving such a testimony is the new hire that has been there for two months.

How easy it is to get caught up with hoping people "like" us. Our innate desire to be connected is glossed over by what we want people to see and, in turn, what we hope they like. I've shared this before, yet so many times I've seen Facebook posts that I know are anything but true. I cherish the posts that are real and authentic. I love the pictures of my family, friends, and loved ones, and following stories of brave children who battle cancer everyday. But, oh, how I cringe at the boastfulness of others.

Over time, I've come to realize that people have a foundational need to be relational, authentic, and transparent. Simply putting on a mask, writing a "boast post," and becoming "known" does not make you a likable person or a good leader. People clicking "like" does not mean people like you. It's all about the need for true authentic relationships at the very core of our being. When that is missing with our family, loved ones, and teams, and even with people we don't know well, success is fleeting.

I looked at Louie, who was determined to win the stare down. "Let's go on a long walk, Lou!" And with that Louie jumped to his feet, happily bounded down the steps, tail wagging, tongue hanging out, and headed toward the door. He is a constant reminder of the need for truth, and from him I have learned how refreshing and freeing the truth can be.

Note: A dear friend of mine recently eulogized her 93-year-old father. In his lifetime, he had lived through the depression and was a hero in World War II. For a man who did not have social media to tout his character, he was honored and well remembered for living a truly authentic life. No truer words were spoken than those from a poem his daughter tearfully read:

The World Needs Men ...

Who cannot be bought.
Whose word is their bond.
Who put character above wealth.
Who are larger than their vocation.
Who do not lose their identity in a crowd.
Who will be as honest in small things as in great things.
Who will make no compromise with wrong.
Whose ambitions are not confined to their own selfish desires.
Who will not say they do it because "everyone else does it."
Who are true to their friends throughout good times and bad...in adversity as well as in prosperity.
Who do not believe that shrewdness and cunning are the best qualities for winning success.
Who are not ashamed to stand for the truth when it is unpopular.
Who can say "no" with emphasis although the rest of the world says "yes."
Robert E. Barnhart, Dad, was that kind of man."

—Lynne Ruhl

4.3 KNOW AND INVEST IN OTHER'S STRENGTHS

I'm sorry to admit it, but we've had a bit of a setback. Louie and I have been working incredibly hard and doing very well. He has improved his greeting when people come to the door, although he did have a "strong" reaction to the guy who was repairing my air conditioner. However, $650 later, I think Louie was on to something, so I let that one go.

Then there was the time he tried to tear down the door to get to the adorable pizza delivery girl. Personally, I don't blame him since Jet's deep-dish pizza was on the other side. Thankfully, he settled down while I was handling the transaction, and was quite well behaved.

But neither of those incidents was the setback. It is much worse and, with apologies to our very capable trainer Zig, I am not sure there's any hope for changing him. You see, he is scared to death of cats. Any color and any type of cat, it doesn't matter...he is terrified. Unfortunately, it does not help that during our walks he can see them skulking across the street, several yards away.

I'm not sure what happened to cause such a strong reaction. It is more than just the normal dog/cat thing. He actually shudders. Evi thinks the nick on his ear is from a cat. How she deducted that, I have no idea, but she may be correct. He relives the deep emotional trauma brought on by a cat in his past every time he sees one, and this has been detrimental to his life's journey—that is, of having fun and happily socializing with other beings in the neighborhood.

But it has occurred to me that Louie has no idea how strong he is. Cat lovers, you may want to stop reading at this point because it won't be pretty. Louie doesn't know that his 40-pound muscular frame could dominate a cat and his mouth is so huge and powerful that one chomp—well, you know where I'm going with this. Yet he doesn't show any signs of aggression toward them; he just whines, shudders, and tries desperately to run away. It's unsettling that he gets so upset and the cat doesn't even acknowledge a dog is in the area. When faced with a feline, he just needs to keep walking, but he feels the need to alert the entire neighborhood that a wicked cat is in the vicinity, and everyone needs to take cover!

Just like Louie, some of us are oblivious to our strengths. We don't know how strong we are in certain areas and what we are truly capable of if we operate out of our strengths. Many of us let fear, doubt, and insecurity rule our minds, and this causes us to miss tapping into our talents. On the other hand, some of us think so highly of ourselves that we overestimate our strengths. And imagine the amount of untapped talent we have within our own team because they are not aware of their strengths.

Many of us have taken assessments that indicate our strengths. These are great tools, but I find the best form of assessment is asking people who will speak truth into my life and give me honest feedback. If you have adult children, ask them to tell you your strengths and weaknesses.

My daughter, Marisa, has always been a wonderful truth teller in my life. Years ago she had to do a high school project about her hero. She read her final report to me and I was impressed with the characteristics she described and the impact this person had in her life. Moreover, I was amazed to learn I was that hero. I certainly did not see myself in that same light, but it inspired me to act out of those strengths.

Some time ago a study was done called "Reflected Best Self Exercise," which is based on research by Robert Quinn, Jane Dutton, Gretchen Spreitzer, and Laura Morgan Roberts. They shared how to go about assessing your strengths by gathering feedback from those around you who know you best.

Many of us are like Louie in that we operate in fear because we don't recognize where we are strong. It has taken me years to identify my strengths and understand how to operate in them. As a leader, my role is to help others recognize their strengths and empower them to cultivate those strengths. I know from experience that helping someone discover their strengths is a blessing, not just for that person, but also to everyone in their sphere of influence.

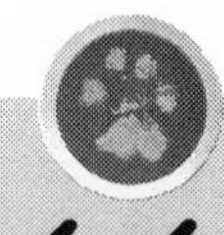

4.4 LEADERS ENCOURAGE OTHERS TO DREAM

One chilly Saturday afternoon, Louie and I were enjoying our favorite things—I was writing, and Louie was napping. As I watched Louie, I noticed he was dreaming. But this was not his usual dream where his legs twitch, and I shake him awake. Instead, his legs were moving in slow motion—almost like he was running gracefully. And rather than his usual abbreviated breaths, he breathed deeply and looked like he was smiling. I watched for several minutes as he kept "running." For a brief moment, I was standing on the sideline watching my pup with a long, sleek body and long stretched out legs, running gracefully around the track as I yelled his name while he neared the finish line. I could hear the theme from *Chariots of Fire* playing in the background. I dared not wake him because he clearly was enjoying the dream.

This reminded me of another runner named Louie, whom I recently read about—Louie Zamperini. Perhaps you've seen the movie or at least heard about his story depicted in *Unbroken.* I read the book first because I think my imagination is better than a Hollywood replication. Though I have yet to see the movie, I understand it is excellent. Louie began his life with very little hope. He was a petty thief and well on his way to a dead-end life of crime. But his older brother saw him run and realized that running might be Louie's way out of his circumstances. Louie ultimately competed in the Olympics held in Munich. He set his sights on the next Olympic games, determined to bring home the gold medal. But all that changed when WWII broke out. It was during those dark days of first being

lost at sea for more than a month and then held prisoner by the Japanese that he began to dream. His dreams actually kept him alive: he remembered what it was like to run and win a race; he dreamed about the next Olympics; he recalled the scent and flavor of his mother's pasta; and he encouraged his fellow prisoners to dream as well.

The human spirit cannot be easily broken, but at times it takes something beyond our own capabilities to dream what may seem impossible. With a clean slate, we may be tempted to be discouraged by dreams that started with a "what if" and faded into a "maybe someday." We must renew our passions and revisit our dreams if we want them fulfilled.

I dreamt long ago of being a writer. In fact, in seventh grade I gave my sister a book of poems only to take them back because I wanted to improve upon them. I've written many stories and worked on projects in my younger days and realized my dream of writing a book could come true. So I started to take the steps to learn how to write well. And, as in any story, there's a villain! A dream slayer, someone who does not want you to realize your dream. They mean well, I suppose. My dream slayer was someone who was incredibly critical of many things, but especially my writing. I am not talking about constructive feedback—we all need that in our lives—rather, this person looked for ways to criticize my writing and then let everyone else know about a mistake I made.

Another dream slayer is our own self-doubt. As the dream begins to formulate and take shape, our minds tell us, "You could never do that," or "You're not that good; no one wants to read your writing." But we have the power to change our thoughts and do away with doubt altogether.

I've also been blessed by people who cast vision for me; those who planted the seeds of a dream before I even saw it. They recognized a talent and passion and encouraged me to follow that dream. One of those people was Ken Blanchard, who loved my book ideas, and eventually endorsed them. I am so thankful he encouraged me to take the next step in realizing my dream. Thankfully, the people who have encouraged my dreams outnumber the ones who have tried to slay them. And similar to Eric Liddell when he referred to running in his famous quote from *Chariots of Fire,* I truly believe I feel God's pleasure when I write.

As leaders, we must be intentional about seeing the talent and passion in others and encourage them to pursue their dreams. Louie Zamperini held onto his dreams and had hope for a better day. That was all he could hold on to, and it helped him survive grueling, inhumane circumstances. We all need to dream and reach beyond our capabilities as it says in one of my favorite verses, "Where there is no vision, the people perish," (Proverbs 29:18). Beware of the dream slayers on your journey. They will disappear as you take the next action step in realizing your dream.

My little Louie finally woke up from his afternoon nap. As his tongue rolled out of his mouth, punctuating a huge yawn, he looked at his paws stretched out in front of him. He looked up at me as if to say, "Mom, I think my legs are just a bit longer, don't you?"

I just shook my head and smiled.

4.5 MIRACLES DO HAPPEN

Investing faith, hope and love in others

Louie and I have been praying for a fellow canine. While I don't believe there are any "ordinary" dogs, this one is quite extraordinary. He is a K-9 Police Officer and we've decided to keep his identity private. He escaped a boarding kennel on December 23 where he was staying while his handler was on vacation.

I first heard about his escape on December 24 on a Cincinnati news station, and have followed the story from various news sources. K9 had a Facebook page, and at the time of his escape there were a few followers, but as word spread, the followers increased. It became clear from the Facebook posts that with the extreme cold, finding K9 quickly was critical. While those of us who followed the story were somewhat emotionally invested, it was nothing like the emotional toll it took on his handler, and I'm sure, K9 himself. For them, sheer determination to find each other became the driving force.

Once the story went viral, a groundswell of support grew. Followers offered support and encouragement, and many volunteers were on foot and in cars searching for K9 with his favorite toy, a tennis ball. He would be spotted here and there, but would run from anyone who got close. Over the two months he was missing, hundreds of people searched, prayed for his safe return, and shed tears over his loss.

Many discussions took place with some who believed he probably hadn't survived or, if he had, might have been taken by someone who didn't realize he was not only a police officer but also a dearly loved companion. Signs were posted and a group of faithful followers prayed every single night at 10 p.m. for K9's protection, safety, and homecoming. Although some gave up on him, his handler and many of us remained optimistic he would be found.

I've been asked why all the emotional upheaval over a dog when there are so many worthy causes to claim our attention. But when people say, "he's just a dog," the mayor of the town responded: "He is not your typical pet. He is a member of and an officer with the Police Department." In a statement to the photographer whose picture of K9 in a field confirmed his final location, the mayor said, "You found an officer who was missing in action and returned him." Clearly, K-9 is more than "just a dog."

Thank goodness this story had a happy ending. After missing for 61 days, K9 was found on a brisk Sunday afternoon. I wept when I read the officer's words: "K9 has been found. I have him in the truck next to me. He's alive and healthy. It's all over finally..." Despite his long absence during one of the coldest winters our area has experienced, K9 lost about 14 pounds, suffered from dehydration, and his paws were fairly reddened by the snow. It's a miracle those were his only ailments.

As the number of followers on Facebook increased, I saw something amazing take place. Right before the news broke that he had been found, there were fewer than 22,000 likes for the K-9's page. By 9 p.m., almost 6,000 additional people viewed and liked K9's page.

Although it's not about the "likes," I wonder why there were so many so quickly. People probably heard about him being lost, but once he was found, they decided to like his page. Why? Because people like happy endings? Perhaps, or is it because people wait to see what happens, hesitant to invest themselves in a story lest they be disappointed if it ends badly. With so much depressing news happening in our world, it is tough to believe in miracles, but they happen all around us, even for our pets.

Miracles don't happen because we wave a magic wand and "poof," we all live happily ever after. They are called miracles because things happen that are out of our control, which result in an ending many times beyond our imagination. There are, however, things we can do to "hasten" miracles:

1. ***Plant the Seed of Faith.*** In this case, a person made one phone call; a volunteer took one more look; a photographer hoped their camera would catch a glimpse of "the hairy kid;" and another offered one more prayer pleading for his safe return. These are seeds of faith that were planted.
2. ***Create an Environment of Hope.*** The "germination" stage for this miracle was hope. The unfailing hope and perseverance of the officer, the police department, the mayor, and all the volunteers and prayer warriors created a fertile environment. And though at times it was by a thread, hope remained strong in the officer's heart.
3. ***Practice the Dynamice Duo of Love and Patience.*** The bond between the officer and K9 was evident and they quickly became our dynamic duo. After we've planted the seeds and created a hopeful environment for it to grow, we come to what is perhaps the hardest part: waiting patiently. What would drive the officer to continue patiently searching every day with no promise of a fruitful outcome? LOVE!

Miracles often happen at the eleventh hour, as in the case of K9. The Sunday he was found was to be the last day of the organized search. The professional tracker and K-9 trainer was set to drive back home, and the trail cameras were being removed.

I had an opportunity to meet the officer, the tracker, and our beloved K9 on his first day back to the station for training. I asked the officer if the reality had taken hold yet. "I still can't believe it," he said shaking his head. "It was truly a miracle. I still wake up in the middle of the night to check his bed to make sure it's real—that he's still there."

I have to wonder, Officer, how many times K9 looks at you with those soulful brown eyes to make sure it's real—that you are still there. It truly is a miracle and will not be quickly forgotten.

4.6

WHAT IS YOUR TRUE IDENTITY

Invest in character building

No matter where Louie and I walk, people stop to talk to him. He is very friendly and loves to engage with people. "What is he?" is the question I'm asked when Louie meets new friends. I give the same answer: "I think he's a Corgi/Beagle mix. And perhaps a little bit of Basset Hound, given his deep bark. He's a rescue, so I'm not totally sure."

They will usually step back and take a long look at my pup. They smile and say, "I can definitely see the Beagle, and perhaps the Corgi as well because of his little legs and long body."

Some people will even share their Corgi or Beagle stories because of the characteristic of each breed. As soon as I say Louie is a Corgi, people will say he must be stubborn. Or when I say that he's a Beagle, they will ask if he howls. This amazes me and causes me to ponder his "true" identity.

So I experimented. When people asked, "What is he?" I responded, "He's the best little buddy ever. He's really well behaved and very loving!"

People look at me as though I didn't hear what they asked. So they clarify their question, "I mean what breed is he?" I understand the desire to discuss breeds, but this tendency has made me aware of how we often do the same thing to people.

When people see me, I wonder how I am identified? Some easily identify me as a woman of Mediterranean descent; some will see me as a bit older—thanks to the white streak in my hair; and some may classify me as middle class, based upon what I may be wearing. Some people take it further and associate me with a political party based on what I look like or what area of town I live in or what church

I attend. Some folks today are simply identified by the company they keep. As I think about it, I'm not sure I want to be identified by any of those things. While I am proud of my heritage and love being a woman, are those the only ways I want to be identified?

This has also made me think about how I look at others. Do I assess the color of their skin or how they dress or what car they drive? Or do I allow others to influence my impression simply based on gossip. Do I identify them by how they treat others, if their words match their actions, if they walk with integrity, and if they are honest, loving, and joyful people?

The words of Martin Luther King, Jr., are still powerful today: "I have a dream that my four little children will one day live in a nation where they will not be judged by the color of their skin, but by the content of their character." One would assume that by now, we would assess people on the content of their characters and not only by what we observe, but just look around at what's going on in our society, and it's clear that is not the case.

Abraham Lincoln said, "Character is like a tree and reputation is like its shadow. The shadow is what we think of it; the tree is the real thing." Our world is desperate for people who act with integrity. But acting with integrity is intentional, and it springs forth from inner character. Unfortunately, what we get is the shadow of a person, not the real thing. We are influenced by our families of origin, our peers, our colleagues, by the people we associate with, and even by the media.

I am doing a study on the characteristics of love, joy, peace, patience, kindness, goodness, faithfulness, gentleness, and self-control with a group of wonderful businesswomen. I have no doubt that by the end of our study we will have grown tremendously, and I hope people will know us by the content of our character. I believe this saying sums it up well: "Don't judge by their appearance or height. People judge by outward appearance, but the Lord looks at the heart."

My hope is that people know my heart based on my character.

As for Louie, he matures more every day. He brings so much joy to others that to identify him only with his breed seems to sell him short and put him in a box. He is more real and honest and true than most people. Our world could learn a thing or two about character from a dog name Lou!

4.7

HIDE AND SEEK

We all play this game

I loved the game hide and seek when I was a child. The neighborhood kids played it almost every night on Cherevilla Lane; hiding behind sheds, perching on branches of large oak trees, and blending in beneath large weeping willow trees. We would start right after supper and play until the streetlights came on. Sometimes we played beyond that if it was a warm summer night and our parents didn't want sweaty kids in the house.

I've noticed Louie also enjoys a good game of hide and seek. Considering how far he has come in the last few years, this particular quirk is endearing and here to stay.

Occasionally I'll give Louie a no-rawhide chewy. He'll start chewing on it for a while and then he'll whine a bit. And then the whine takes on another tone as he searches throughout the house for a safe place to bury the chewy. Sometimes that place is in my granddaughter's room. Sometimes it's behind the couch. But many times it's within the folds of a blanket on his couch. I don't believe it's a matter of actually hiding the chewy, as much as it is that he loves to find the chewy. He does this every single time.

I recently noticed that as he was burying his chewy, he was very careful not to let me see him. It's all part of the game. Then when I ask where his chewy is, his ears perk up and he is ready to play a little game of hide and seek. I am somewhat amazed that he isn't more protective as I get close to the hiding spot, but rather he looks toward the spot as if to say, "Don't look over there, Mom. It's not there."

The excitement mounts as I draw closer and closer, and voilà. There's the chewy. He loves it when *I find the chewy and we celebrate that he's such a smart boy.*

The game continues as long as he has a chewy to hide. I don't know what it is about this hide and seek game that we all love so much. As adults we still play that game, but with a slight twist. We still hide certain things in our lives that we don't want people know about, because we fear it could ruin the relationship. We don't want people to know certain things because we fear they might think negatively about us. Yet deep down we all want to be exposed with the hope that when we are found, we will still be loved and accepted. We all seek authenticity and truth. It's a hunger within all of us, and there is freedom in being who we truly are, not what the world thinks we should be.

When we take off our masks and stop hiding, the authentic "us" is revealed. Some people will appreciate and honor that, while others won't. Good leaders help people come out from their hiding places and seek authenticity. To do that, we must:

1. Be intentional about building trust.
2. Demonstrate authenticity in our own lives.
3. Provide a safe place and be a safe person for people to be real.

As for Louie, when I find the little treasure that he's hidden, he seems to do a celebration dance, as if the unveiling bonds us even closer. Every one has a treasure within them. Seek to help people uncover their treasures, and you will create a culture of trust and love, where people can be productive and effective.

4.8 WE DON'T ALWAYS CHOOSE WHOM WE LEAD

But we can choose how we behave!

"Why did you get that dog anyway?" a friend asked as we were eating, exasperated with Louie who had finally settled down after attacking her at the door. "He's so different from what you've been used to." She was referring to my previous pets, two Bichons and a Cocker Spaniel.

Good question, I thought to myself. Why did I adopt this seemingly docile pup that turned out to be anything but sweet and gentle? As I'm typing, he is trying to "bury" his chewy toy behind the sofa in the family room, and I have to shake my head and wonder. I've been accustomed to soft and fluffy, somewhat dainty, little dogs. There is nothing soft and fluffy about Louie, and certainly nothing dainty! And on days where the temperature is –5 degrees and we have to "go" outside, I have to ask why?

Well, I love him, first and foremost. And I did choose him, and it was not an emotional decision. As he regally sat in his crate at the adopt-a-pet weekend, I noticed he had character and a presence. I knew he needed me…and I needed him. That's not how we typically select our employees, but sometimes when we accept a leadership position, there are people we lead whom we would like to help find other jobs. We shake our heads and wonder why on earth they are part of our team.

<<<

DOING MY BEST TO LEAD THIS FILM CREW EVEN THOUGH I HAD NOTHING TO DO WITH THEM BEING HERE

<<<

They may not act in familiar ways, they may seem a bit quirky, and there are probably days we wish they would simply resign. Then we start seeing signs of hope, we genuinely give affirmations and suddenly, we see improvement—ever so slight—but it's there. We notice their contributions to the team, and our one-on-one times are more fulfilling. We notice that they have hidden exceptional characteristics and potential, even though they lack what *we* believe they need in order to be an exceptional employee.

Just like Louie, some people we lead are diamonds in the rough. They appear very ordinary at first glance, and their true beauty as jewels is only realized through a very difficult process. A good leader is often faced with the dilemma of either taking time to invest in a person or deciding it's time to let them go.

I believe every interaction we have with another human being has a purpose. And when I find myself spending time with someone because our roles intertwine, I must take a look at how I can best invest in this person's life. I am willing to invest in others who:

1. Show genuine interest in professional and personal growth.
2. Have a sense of self awareness and a personal vision.

3. Are open to and welcome feedback, coaching and mentoring.
4. Are committed to learning.
5. Are willing to take risks.
6. Possess self-management skills.

As leaders we must be willing to invest in others, especially those who are so different from our expectations. Sometimes we toss people aside because they don't meet our needs or measure up to our standards. A good leader recognizes that some people are placed in our life for the very purpose of refining us. Are we willing to give them our time and invest in them? I realize there are times we do need to help others find another job, but most times it takes a refining process to bring out the best in others and ourselves.

Louie is still burying his chewy and I am still shaking my head. I don't mind spending time pouring into him because I see the potential and personality, and I am the richer person for giving away my heart and my time!

4.9

HIT "PAWS": LOUIE'S JOY AND GRATITUDE

I wish I could capture the look on Louie's face and his body language as we walk. I know I can snap a picture or even take a video, but neither would do his joy justice. You see, a picture, while it paints a thousand words, still does not truly capture the moment of pure bliss for my pup. He loves to walk and it is obvious. He loves to dig in the dirt, to greet people along the way, and breathe in new smells. I can tell it fills his heart with joy.

Other than a bit of time, it doesn't cost me a cent to provide this joyful experience for Louie. I know he appreciates our walks just by his enthusiastic reaction to my picking up his leash.

Louie's joy and gratitude cause me to hit the PAWS button and ask: how thankful am I for the simple pleasures in life? I am blessed with an awesome family that I love and who loves me. I live in a great country, and have wonderful friends, and can use the gifts God has given me. Rather than focusing on negative issues and problems, I choose to focus on joy! The first step in choosing happiness is to be thankful.

Studies have shown that people are happier and more joyful when they are grateful. The benefits of being grateful are nearly endless. People who regularly practice gratitude by taking time to notice and reflect upon the things they're thankful for experience more positive emotions, feel more alive, sleep better, ex-

press more compassion and kindness, and even have stronger immune systems. Take time to PAWS and remember all there is to be thankful for, especially the relationships and the simple things.

4.10 IS THERE A DOG IN THE HOUSE?

Invest in developing others

The memory of my first few weeks with Louie brings a smile to my face! We almost didn't have a "first few weeks together" because of his challenging behaviors, but we pressed through.

When he first came to live with me, he would roam around my house, sniffing and whining. I wondered if he needed to go outside, so I would take him out, let him do his thing, and then bring him back in. A few minutes later, he would run upstairs and then downstairs, whining. "Again?" I thought to myself. "Does he have to go out again? What's with this dog?" He whined constantly and seemed to be searching for something, anything, familiar to him.

My visit with Louie to the vet, Dr. Paul, for his first health checkup was interesting. When Dr. Paul checked him, Lou whined and shook with fear, but the vet just kept going. "He's a pretty healthy pup. Any issues that you notice?"

"Yes! He whines! Incessantly! I'll be working in my office and Louie will be checking out my home. He'll pop into my office, look around, whine, and go back through the house, whining, whining, constantly whining."

"Well," said Dr. Paul, "don't let him run loose through your home. When you're not there, crate him, and when you are there, keep him close to you. But don't let him run through your home."

"Okay," I thought, "that's simple enough." Because I work from home, I made a bed for him right under my desk and blocked the stairway to the upstairs level. I kept a close watch on him and interacted with him when I was able to do so. Amazingly, his whining and desire to roam around the house stopped, and the sighs and active dreams of a happy pup filled my office.

All Louie needed was a little watchful supervision. He needed to know I was close by. He needed to understand his boundaries and just how far he could safely explore without wandering too far away or getting lost.

Isn't this just like our teams? When they first engage with our organizations, we think we are doing them a favor by letting them "roam." They spend their time "onboarding" or looking around for anything that looks familiar to them, which could cause frustration. Like Louie, they just need a little watchful supervision. They need to know their leader is close by and available when needed. They need to understand what their boundaries are and that if they make a mistake, it is OK because, hopefully, the problem is easy to rectify.

This section of the LOUIE leadership model is "I" for *investment.* The time that I poured into helping Louie build trust and confidence and making him feel safe was an investment. It took some time, but the investment was worth every minute. Leader, you will never regret investing the necessary time and tools in your team to build trust and help them feel safe and to know they are valued.

As I type this chapter, I have no idea where Louie is. He's in my house but not under my feet. In fact, he is never under my feet these days. Many times I stand by my front door, hands on my hips, loudly asking, "Is there a dog in the house?" No answer. "Any dog? Is there any dog in the house?" No answer. "Is there any dog in the house who would like to go for a walk?" With that, I hear the rumblings of four squatty little legs running to the front door from any one of his favorite places. He is either upstairs, looking out over his kingdom through the second story window, downstairs in his crate (voluntarily), or out on the deck, sunning himself. He has developed enough that he no longer needs my watchful supervision. He trusts that if anything changes, I'll inform him. For now, he's just fine—wherever he is!

4.11

YOUR MOST IMPORTANT INVESTMENT

Reignite your sense of wonder

Louie hit a rough patch last week. One night shortly after settling into our nightly routine, he became restless. He rarely dances around to signal his need to go outside; when he did so, we made it to the front yard just in the nick of time. He clearly had an upset stomach and was one miserable little pup.

I wasn't sure how he would fare through the night, but I knew he would let me know if he needed to make a trip outside. Sure enough, at midnight and then again at 1:30 a.m., he woke me up, needing to go out. I was administering the proper foods to settle his digestive system, but I had already decided to call the vet in the morning to get him in as soon as possible.

Then something magical happened. It's tough to put the words "magical" and "upset stomach" in the same sentence, but that is exactly what took place. While I was thinking through all the practical reasons Louie was sick and slowly trying to coax him back into the house, he stopped and looked far off into the distance. Normally, Louie can become nervous when he's outside in the dark; he usually wants to head back inside as soon as possible. Our trainer has advised me that I need to walk boldly and with confidence when we're outside after dark so that Louie will feel safe.

But standing outside at 1:30 in the morning, I had no desire to be the alpha. I just wanted to go back to bed with a hope and a prayer that Louie would be on the mend. At the moment, though, Louie was fixated on something that grabbed his attention; even with a slight tug, he would not move.

Then it happened. Rather than scurrying back to the safety of the house, we stood and took in the magic of a peaceful, quiet night. He slowly looked from the street up to the stars above. I stopped, too, and looked. The sky was beautiful, and the quietness with a few faint nighttime sounds was breathtaking. Louie seemed to marvel at the night sky. I noticed it, too—and it grabbed my heart.

We spent a long moment drinking in the beauty. I looked at my pup, and we both knew it was time to go in. After our midnight reverie, whatever Louie tapped into must have healed his nerves because he settled in for a long, deep sleep. The next day, he woke up without a trace of sickness.

As I type out this message, I am compelled to ponder this thought: when did I lose this sense of wonder? I see it emerge when I play with my grandchildren—when we go off on adventures. But as Louie and I stood together that evening, I realized that it can be easy to mistake wonder for foolishness. In fact, I have to ask myself—is this thought just foolishness?

I so desire to reignite my sense of incredible marvel. For me, this is about more than being creative: it is seeing the beauty and magic in the world all around us—the creation that God breathed life into. It is engaging with a dear friend in deep, heartwarming conversation. It is watching my beautiful niece walk along a peaceful garden path to join her soon-to-be-husband in their outdoor wedding ceremony. It is witnessing the miraculous birth of my grandchildren. It is running outside to catch the ice cream truck as it passes through my neighborhood—and having my brother and his family joining me, which happened just last week. Four adults standing in my driveway, eagerly anticipating the thrill of eating ice cream from a truck, unprompted by children!

Admit it—we yearn to be moved by seeing things beyond our physical world. We all want to feel profoundly alive, to feel like we're a part of the grander scheme of things. Yet many of us have lost this sense of curiosity. Moments that might have taken our breath away from our younger selves now may not move us at all.

<<<

MY ALPHA PUPS MAKE THE BEST COOKIES

<<<

If you are a leader in an organization, community, or family, what are ways you could reignite your sense of wonder? Perhaps you feel aware that you've lost it, or perhaps you still do experience it. What about those you lead—do you see glimpses of their capacity for awe? The greatest gift you can give to others is to help them navigate uncertain waters and enter that new world with them. You can choose to intentionally engage in conversations with your team about recapturing this magical sense. You and your team may be surprised by feeling powerfully impacted as you tap into this sense.

I hope Louie never losses his sense of awe. I am not saying that he has this down, or even that he is cognizant of his tender sense of wonder. Nevertheless, I envy his ability to stop and connect with creation and draw from that a sense of peace. Even on that night without sleep, unexpected and moving lessons were shown to me by my pup, Louie.

Section Five

EMPOWER OTHERS

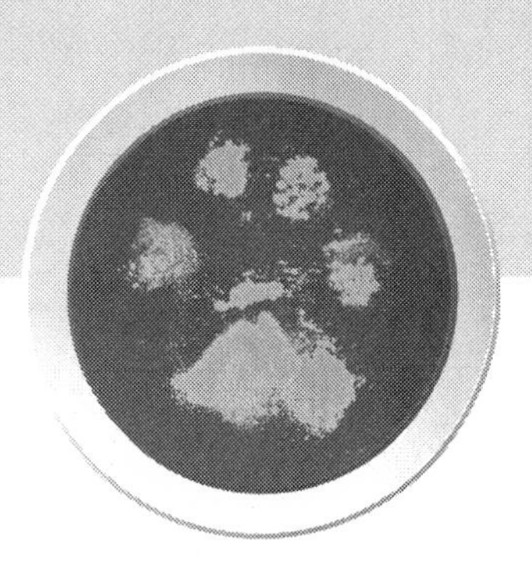

"As we look ahead into the next century,
leaders will be those who empower others."
—Bill Gates

Louie is an entirely different dog today because I love him. I took the time to set up a development plan and was clear about objectives and goals for him to be a good, healthy dog and for us to enjoy a relationship together. I had to understand his needs. I had to understand his background. I had to figure out what was going on with him. I invested time, my skill set, and other people's skill sets to help develop him. He is empowered to be a fun-loving, free little dog.

The last step in my leadership training with Louie was to empower him. Empowering your team is essential, but it's not just letting people do whatever they want to do. Empowering is taking the time to love them and establishing clear objectives and goals. It is understanding them, and investing in them. Once you do these things, your people will be empowered to use their gifts and talents to do their jobs; and in doing so, you empower them to be the people they were created to be—not who you think they should be. They will be loved and valued.

My work with Louie is not unlike leading our teams. Transformation occurs when we apply the LOUIE leadership model: **L**ove, **O**bjectives, **U**nderstanding, **I**nvestment, and **E**mpowerment, as well as the PAWS model: **P**ause, **A**sk, **W**isdom, and **S**top and **S**eek. Throughout *Lead Like Louie,* you will see more examples of these two models wrapped in stories of love, struggles, and immense joy.

While it brings me great pleasure to know that Louie is a transformed dog, I believe I am the one who has been profoundly changed into a better leader and a better person because of the lessons I've learned from a little adopted dog named Louie.

5.1

I'M NOT JUMPING THROUGH HOOPS ANYMORE!

Don't micro-manage—Empower!

I've noticed Louie has an odd habit when we walk. He walks on the street curb like he is walking on a balance beam. And he's quite good! In fact, many times he will run on the curb and not miss a beat. I joked with our trainer, Zig, that we should get Louie into agility training. Zig kindly reminded me that Louie would need more obedience training before he could handle an agility class.

It was wise advice, but curiosity got the better of me. I looked into a place that has an easy-to-use obstacle course where dogs chase a lead through tunnels and over bars, and they don't need prior training. So my six-year-old granddaughter, Evi, joined Louie and me as we checked out this fun adventure.

It was obvious from the start that Louie would have nothing to do with chasing a silly lead on a wire aimed at getting him to jump or run. I'm sure if the lead had a treat on it, he might have been persuaded, but that was not part of the plan. So Evi jumped into the ring and started running with him, and the two of them had a blast. That lasted one cycle until his attention went elsewhere. Evi tried to get him to chase her, but Louie was done. He clearly was not going to jump through any more hoops and, in fact, desperately tried to find a way to escape.

And escape he did. He found a small opening in the fence and took off running through the outside area that didn't appear to be enclosed. Zig told me never to chase Louie if he gets loose because he'll think it's a game, but I was afraid of what could happen if he ran into the busy street. As Louie's ears flapped in the wind and his tongue hung out to the side, the chase was on. I jumped over a small fence and ran at high speed to tackle him and bring him safely back into the ring. I did all this while yelling at Evi to stay put because I didn't want to worry about her as well, but she was too enthralled by the sight of my running and jumping that she wasn't going anywhere.

As we were driving home, I asked Louie, "Why did you run away from me? Don't you realize if you run away I will not be behind you? You'll be lost! Don't you remember what it was like being on the streets all alone?" Evi chimed in with a sad face, "Yeah, Louie, that was scary. Don't ever do that again!" I smiled as I looked at my pup through the rear view mirror, his tongue still hanging out and a big smile on his face as though he had achieved a major accomplishment, and I added "But I can't blame you, Lou! I don't like to jump through hoops either." Louie sat regally, staring out the window as we drove in silence toward home.

As I reflected on that incident, I realized that Louie was not going to jump through hoops or run around a path and, like most humans, he looked for the quickest escape route. I was reminded of an organization I once worked with that was one of the most toxic cultures I had ever experienced because the leader expected the employees to jump through hoops on a continual basis. What made it so toxic was that the image portrayed to the public was completely different than that of the actual culture. Every employee walked on eggshells out of fear of the employer and they knew that if they spoke the truth, they could be out of a job.

Over the years, I have seen and heard about many toxic workplaces. How do you know when a culture is toxic and a leader is self-serving? It is not so easy to determine just by observing. It takes experiencing the culture and often, by the time the determination is made, the damage is done. But here are some signs:

- People are afraid to be themselves and honest conversations are a rarity.
- The leader works hard at displaying a perfect image outside the organization and "talks" about how great the culture is.
- There is a revolving door of employees (turnover numbers can be masked).
- There is a pattern of disgruntled employees and broken relationships.

- The team picture changes every year because the team is totally different every year.
- When employees leave, relationships end (heaven forbid the outside world truly know what's going on inside).
- Employees are nervous and stop trying to please the leader because they know nothing ever will.
- Words of affirmation are rarely given.
- The leader only shares stories that cast him or her in a positive light.
- There are small blips of successes here and there but over all, growth is stagnant.
- They cultivate an image to hide their insecurities and fears.
- A self-serving leader reads this list and says, "Thank goodness I'm nothing like that."
- The servant leader reads this list and says, "But for the grace of God, there go I!"

I could go on, but I'm sure you get the picture. There are many wonderful leaders who have a servant's heart, and care more for others than themselves. And because they are servant leaders, their businesses continue to enjoy sustainable growth, and employees are recognized for their part in the success. Their employees enjoy going to work in the morning instead of getting that knotted feeling every Sunday evening because of what they have to face on Monday. The best servant leaders are those who have removed their egos, and are authentic and other-focused. Be intentional about being a servant leader.

As for Louie...well, we'll work on his agility. I believe Zig was right that he needs a bit more obedience training. Ok, he needs *much more obedience training!*

5.2

LOUIE, YOU'RE FIRED

The need to end well

Louie is a superstar in his training class, and he actually understands his training commands at home. He welcomes guests when they enter my home—thanks to training him with a delicious special treat—and sits patiently while they enter. He waits to be released and then slowly examines my guests, starting at their feet. He's learned not to jump, although he get excited and must be reminded constantly to settle down.

Despite the amount of time and work we've invested, he has one consistently bad behavior. Once someone is settled in at the table or on the couch, if they make a move to go into the kitchen or the bathroom, he will charge after them. Obviously, this is unacceptable behavior! No one believes Louie does this until they see it happen.

Louie and I have discussed this problem: we have asked neighbors to practice with us; I have been extremely firm with him when he goes after guests; and finally I've removed him from the activity. Yet this behavior persists.

I know he is being territorial, and I attribute it to the fact that he has it so good here that he doesn't want to share it. But at this point, if Louie were my employee, I would fire him!

Or would I?

Many times our star performers demonstrate a consistently bad behavior, and we make excuses for them. We ignore the bad behavior as long as they continue to perform. In addition, we will excuse the behavior of others who aren't perform-

<<<

THEY CAN'T FIRE ME!
I VOLUNTEER TO GO SEE MY PALS
AT BUFFALO WINGS & RINGS

<<<

ing simply because we love them. Basically, we avoid disengaging with employees because it is never easy and it almost always gets ugly.

I had a friend who was in the process of disengaging with an employee. "We must end this well," were his words and they resonated with my heart. Not very many leaders care about ending well. They want to eliminate the "poison" as quickly as possible and finally have a good team.

This reminded me of the saying, "All's well that ends well." Endings are necessary, but a "good" ending is essential. Even if things have not gone well, ending a relationship (whether it's personal or professional) in a positive and growth-promoting way can repair things.

Often we recognize that an ending is imminent, but instead of doing the hard work to end things well, we lapse into fear, insecurity, and pride, which leads to a reactionary response. Sometimes quick terminations are best but, even then, seeking to end things well is necessary in order to benefit everyone involved, even other employees.

What does ending well look like? Without getting into human resource debates, each individual situation should be handled differently. I'd like to challenge leaders, that is if it is clear that an employee is not the best fit for the position, then they need to have an honest conversation about it. This is, of course, risky, but it is better than turning into the Queen (or King) of Hearts, wielding an axe, and yelling, "Off with their head," because someone shared their feelings about things not working out. It is important to always end well. It is not easy, but for the sake of your culture, it is very important. When it's possible, preserve the personal relationship even if the professional one has to end. This goes for friendships, too. Don't burn bridges, and try to avoid bitterness and regret when relationships evolve.

Since this is a dog book, I've also reflected on the end of life for all of my pups. How do you end well? It is heart wrenching to take that last drive to the vet and carry them in your arms, knowing it will be the last time you hold them. As tough as that decision was for each dog I've loved, I knew when it was time. I made sure I was nose to nose with my pup so they could look into my eyes as their life slowly slipped away. I wanted them to know they were deeply loved, and I was intentional about ending well.

As for Louie, of course, I will not be firing him any time soon so I'm not accepting requests for his resume at this time. He does make office visits and is a stellar dog in the workplace. And you are welcome to come to my home any-time...at your own risk!

5.3

LOUIE, THE HALL MONITOR

Empowered to protect

Louie's relationship with my granddaughters is indescribable. The words, "Sissy's coming," barely pass my lips when he high tails it to the kitchen window and whines as he waits for his two "sissys" to make their appearances.

To say he loves them is an understatement. He adores them, and I think he feels responsible for their safety. So recently, after the big welcome with hugs around his neck and sloppy dog kisses, we were in for a very fun evening at Nonna's!

A few minutes into our time together, I received a text from my daughter letting me know she had forgotten to send the monitor. I replied, "No worries. Louie will be the hall monitor tonight." I'm sure my daughter shook her head and smiled at the thought of Louie "monitoring" Mea and Evi.

There was a time when Louie had to stay in a pen so he would not rush the girls when they would "sneak" into my bedroom for our morning snuggles. Now, he sleeps on a nice, cushy bed on the floor next to mine. On this particular night, I decided to try something different. I kept the doors open so he could wander into their room and sleep. I even put his first floor bed next to their beds, just in case.

As we enjoyed movies and popcorn, Louie decided to crawl into his own bed in my room. He was fast asleep by the time the girls settled into their beds. After we read several books and exchanged hugs and kisses, I finally declared, "Time for everyone, Nonna included, to go to bed." Sometime during the night, I woke up and looked over the edge of my bed to see that Louie was no longer in his sleeping area. Typically he is not a roamer—once he goes to bed, he stays in bed—so

I knew exactly where he was. I tiptoed down the hallway to the girls' room and there was my little buddy, sound asleep on his bed on the floor, right by Mea and Evi's beds. They were sound asleep, no doubt feeling safe in Nonna's home with their watch dog, Louie! I fell back to sleep until morning when all three little bodies entered my room, ready for their morning snuggles.

It wasn't that long ago that Louie needed reassurance that my home was a safe place. Now, he ensures it is a safe place for his girls. Feeling safe is one of our greatest needs. This holds true in all areas of life. One of the greatest responsibilities leaders have is creating a safe environment where trust is cultivated, people respect each other, and boundaries are honored. When people feel safe, they are free to let their guard down. They work harder and are more productive.

Sadly, some leaders are more concerned with their images and what people think of them than they are about creating an environment of safety. This creates an unstable environment where people are guarded. Typically, employees don't stay long in such a place.

Ask yourself: Am I a safe leader? You might consider conducting a "safety inventory" of your organization and your relationships. Ask your colleagues, employees and friends if they consider you and your environment safe.

Louie's role is to enjoy the safety of his home and to make sure his girls are safe when they are there. His peaceful demeanor indicates the need for safety was high on his list, right next to his need for love. And he gets plenty of that in our home!

5.4

ENVY—A VERY DEADLY SIN

An obstacle to empowerment

There's a new boy in the neighborhood, and Louie is not happy. Although Lou loves when a new gal pal moves in, he is not very fond of this little pup, Big Mac.

Life was going along just fine for Louie. Everybody loves on him when they see him, and they pay attention when they hear him whine for their attention as we walk. He gladly accepts invitations into other people's homes, and thoroughly enjoys running around the yard with his buddy, Mick. And then came Mac. Mac is seven pounds of fluffy white and brown hair and super power energy. Everyone thinks he's adorable…except Lou.

At first, Louie was okay with the idea of a new dog in town. He checked out Mac via the smells he left in his owner's front yard, and Louie was intrigued. Then Lou saw him from a distance and things seemed fine. But when they met face to face, Lou immediately ran the other way. Mac had too much energy and in-your-face action. Mac's mom and I gave them time to warm up to each other, but one afternoon I noticed something. Louie was particularly clingy to Mac's mom, as though he needed reassurance that she still loved him. Then Lou gave Mac a quick snarl as a warning and went off to play with another dog he has known for some time.

Oh, the dreadful feeling of envy that slithers almost unnoticeably into our hearts. We've all experienced it. It usually creeps in with its pal, comparison, and causes resentment of what we perceive as someone else's advantage—in Louie's

case it was the serious cuteness of another pup, resulting in lots of attention from everyone.

I thought about this in regards to the common leadership adage to surround yourself with those who are smarter than you. What is *not* part of that quote is to be sure to check your level of confidence. Many leaders say they are looking for others who can be a great addition to their teams, but then squelch any opportunity for the new person to actually use their skills for fear it may outshine them. Those leaders will find acceptable ways of expressing their resentment by using the big "but" approach—"He may be a good sales person, BUT he doesn't have a clue how to write a decent proposal." Or sometimes we question someone's motive because we are actually envious toward them.

I once read a story[1] of two men, both of whom were seriously ill and occupied the same small hospital room. One man was allowed to sit up in his bed for an hour each afternoon to help drain the fluid from his lungs. His bed was next to the room's only window. The other man had to spend all his time flat on his back.

The men talked for hours about everything. Each afternoon, when the man in the bed by the window could sit up, he would pass the time by describing to his roommate all the things he could see outside the window. The man in the other bed would live for those one-hour periods when his world came alive because his

[1]Swindoll, Charles R. *The Tale of the Tardy Oxcart,* 1998.

roommate described a park with a lake, on which birds swam and by which children played. Although the other man could not hear any of the sounds, he could see them in his mind's eye as the gentleman by the window beautifully described all the activity.

That is, until envy slithered in: "Why should he have all the pleasure of seeing everything while I never get to see anything?" It wasn't fair. At first, the man felt ashamed because he enjoyed the man's friendship and thoughtful descriptions of what was going on outside the window. But as the days passed, his envy eroded into resentment. He began to brood, and he found himself unable to sleep. He should be the one by that window—and that thought controlled his life.

Late one night, as he lay staring at the ceiling, the man by the window began to cough. He was choking on the fluid in his lungs. The other man watched in the dimly lit room as the struggling man by the window groped for the button to call for help. Listening from across the room, he never moved, never pushed his own button, which would have brought the nurse running. In less than five minutes the coughing and choking stopped, along with the sound of breathing.

Now there was only silence—deadly silence. The following morning the day nurse arrived to bring water for their baths. When she found the lifeless body of the man by the window, she was saddened and called the hospital attendants to take it away—no words, no fuss. As soon as it seemed appropriate, the other man asked if he could be moved next to the window. The nurse was happy to make the switch, and after she was sure he was comfortable, she left him alone. Slowly, painfully, he propped himself up on one elbow to take his first look. Finally, he would have the joy of seeing it all himself. He strained to look out the window beside the bed and found it faced a blank wall.

Envy is indeed a deadly sin, and more pervasive in leadership than we think. If we as leaders are not careful, we can allow envy to kill spirits and damage our team's morale.

As for Louie and Big Mac, I am sure Louie will learn to love Mac—all in due time!

5.5 LIFELONG FRIENDS

True empowerment

I've written about Louie's new gal pals moving into the neighborhood, Louie getting to know rambunctious puppies, and his tolerance (or occasional intolerance) of guests in our home. You've been introduced to his chest-bumping pal, Mick, his walking buddy Sully, and his steady girls Eve and Ellie. But we've not talked about Sampson much. That's because there's not much to talk about. Sampson (or Sammy) is just a steady-as-you-go, no drama kind of pup. And Louie loves that because Louie needs steady and stable.

Louie and Sammy met a few years ago. Sampson is an adorable pug who is occasionally stubborn while walking with his mom. But Louie rarely sees that side of Sammy. The pups happily acknowledge each other and then just walk side by side. Sammy waddles, Louie prances, and the pace seems to work for them both.

Lou can be who he is when he's with Sampson. He can just simply be. It's almost as though he lets out a long sigh and says, "Hey buddy." And then they just walk together. They don't romp around or chase each other. They just stroll.

While I have many friends and family members who love me just as I am, my lifetime friend, Gina, has known me since the day I was born. Our parents were friends long before we came along, and despite their moving to L.A. when Gina and I were three, our parents remained friends and my friendship with Gina deepened over the years. To this day, Gina and I talk regularly and visit as often as possible.

<<<
MY LIFELONG PAL, GINA
<<<

The best thing about Gina is that I can be my authentic self with her. I don't have to perform or jump through hoops or pretend or walk on egg shells. I learned about the power of vulnerability decades ago because my friendship with Gina helped me see the areas in my life that kept me from being real. It wasn't a book or a training session or a counselor, although those are great tools. It was the power of relationship that brought me to where I am today.

Much like Louie and Sampson, Gina and I don't have to be talking to feel close, we can simply bask in the golden silence of true friendship. We have shared life's sorrows, including death of loved ones, divorce, and remarriage. And we've also shared life's joys, such as the birth of each other's children. We can call at 3 a.m. and one of us will answer the phone with, "What's wrong?" We've been through sickness, job promotions, sixty birthdays, and many Kauai sunsets. Through thick and thin, we will always be best friends.

I know Gina loves me enough to address a character flaw she may see in me long before others do. I trust her to be honest and caring, so I welcome her feedback. Some leaders think they are above feedback, but without it they can end up with negative consequences that affect their relationships, as well as their job performance. We all need friends in our lives who act as a stopgap to our bad behavioral choices. And we must be willing to listen.

Every leader needs a Gina! And every leader needs to hear when their Gina says, "I'm not sure about that." Just as every Louie needs a Sampson, a steady-as-you-go, let's walk side-by-side pal who cares more about you than they do themselves. These kinds of friends truly empower us, enrich our lives, and make us better people, leaders...or pets!

5.6

LOUIE AND I HAVE SOMETHING IN COMMON: WE'RE BOTH INTROVERTS

Empowering others to use their energy wisely

Recently I was thinking of getting another dog. Louie is home alone so often, and I worry he gets lonely when I'm not around. He gets plenty of exercise thanks to Sully and his mom, but he's a pack animal, and I don't think I'm enough "pack" for him.

But then I remember my first doggie duo. My daughter Marisa and I were convinced that Buffy, the first dog we owned together, was lonely and needed a buddy. So we brought a very energetic Bichon puppy named Bree home when Buffy was 3-years-old…she was Buffy's worst nightmare.

Then after Buffy died, we adopted Cece. Cece wanted me all to herself, which was not going to happen as long as Bree was around. After they passed within three years of each other, I took a break from any more doggie drama. And now there's Louie!

But I noticed something interesting about Louie. He loves his buddies and will whine to go out to play, but when he's done, he comes home and quietly goes to his man cave. He has a spot in my bedroom and a crate on the lower level of my home and he prefers that no one invade his privacy. After observing his behavior over the last few years, it is clear he loves to be alone. Even when I'm home, he is not under my feet. He will go into his crate while I am working or go to his favorite spot to look out the window.

Perhaps this is a learned behavior after living with me since 2013. I love to be alone. I enjoy the quietness of my home, and I reenergize by spending time alone. I plan for plenty of white space on my calendar for that purpose. I guard that time because it is precious to me. I would never be able to pour into people as I do if I did not have plenty of time alone.

The reactions I receive when I tell people I'm an introvert ranges from utter disbelief to acknowledgement that they catch a glimpse of introversion occasionally. The audiences I speak to are usually the ones who display disbelief, because their idea of an introvert is not someone who is comfortable giving speeches. I learned many years ago from my friend Lynne, the primary difference between an introvert and an extrovert. She asked one simple question: "You've been around people all day at work or at a social event. Upon arriving home you receive a call from a friend who invites you to a party. Would you turn around and head out to the party or politely decline to stay home?" I didn't hesitate…stay home!

She explained that it doesn't mean I am shy or socially awkward or even afraid of public speaking. It simply means I recharge by being alone.

The terms extrovert and introvert refer to the ways people use their energy. These words have psychological meaning that is different from the way they are used in everyday language. Everyone spends some time extroverting and some time introverting. Don't confuse introversion with shyness or reclusiveness. They are not related and I am far from shy.

And things get really tricky when you throw in a new term: *ambivert*—a word used to describe someone who exhibits qualities of both introversion and extroversion. Stop it! I'm an introvert who functions quite well in an extroverted world, and I love my time alone.

Good leaders understand that people have differing ways of directing their energies. Not everyone will respond the same way, even in the same situations. Have your extroverted employees that have winning others over (WOO) as a strength go to the social networking events. Be aware of what energizes and what drains you, your loved ones, and employees.

I sometimes wonder if the superficiality of our culture today, thanks to social media, hasn't made me more keenly aware of being introverted. As someone who is very relational, my connection with others is key to my well-being. Yet I still prefer time alone, rather than engage in any insincere or phony relationship. And now I have an introverted dog that lives with me, and I'm thankful we are so compatible. He makes coming home even more of a welcome reprieve.

5.7

LOUIE IS A CREATURE OF HABIT

Getting past "We've always done it this way"

Louie is such a creature of habit. He sleeps until I awake, then he jumps on the bed when I call him for morning snuggles, after which he heads down to the kitchen for his breakfast, back upstairs to watch out the window, then goes on a walk after I've showered and dressed (this is all before 7a.m.). His days are mixed with whatever my schedule includes. Sometimes that means long walks, a visit to the park, or visits with my granddaughters. Other times are spent in his cozy crate (whether I'm home working or out) and an afternoon walk with Sully. He has dinner, then an evening walk and play time, and he's off to bed at 8:30 p.m.—no matter what is going on in my home.

I'll change our walking pattern and even then he will stand at the crossroad and wait to see what direction I'll go and then happily trot off in that direction. His habits make him feel comfortable, and given his past, I am happy to accommodate him.

I have to laugh when I watch his quirky little ways. I am reminded of a story I heard long ago from Zig Ziglar. A young bride was cooking dinner for her husband. He watched her carefully season the roast and then proceed to cut off one end, and then the other end. He asked his wife why she cut off the ends of the roast. She replied that her mother had always done it that way and that was reason enough for her. Since the wife's mother was visiting, they asked her why she always cut off the end of the roast. Mother replied that this was the way her mother did it. Mother, daughter, and son-in-law then decided to call grandmother and solve this three-generation mystery. Grandmother promptly replied that she cut the end of the roast because her roaster was too small to cook it in one piece.

We do things a certain way because we've always done them that way and, quite honestly, we're comfortable with that. But is that always the best way? Not necessarily. Regardless of who originally penned this saying, whether Albert Einstein, Henry Ford, or perhaps Mark Twain, these words still ring true today: "If you always do what you've always done, you will always get what you've always got." Many work environments today are stuck in the "We've always done it that way" syndrome, with no end in sight.

History and tradition are necessary for a rich working environment where people learn how the business started and how it has grown. And many processes are in place because of the hours put into finding just the right workflow. However, many ideas are tossed to the wayside because a leader or leaders cannot see that though something might have worked in the past, there are possibilities to make a change for the better going forward. Even worse, sometimes our prejudices are based on "We've always [voted, practiced, treated people] that way" in the past, and we're not self-aware enough to break out of that thinking.

The key to breaking through this barrier is *trust*! When I challenge Louie to do things a different way, he trusts me enough to comply. He may look at me as if to say, "Are you sure?" or "Is this the way, really?" But he carries on because he trusts me.

If leaders are secure in their roles and they exude trust with their team and vice versa, the culture breeds openness and spontaneity of new ideas. The next time there's even a hint of "We've Always Done It This Way" (WADITW), carefully consider the following steps:

- ***Stop*** before saying another word and take a deep breath!
- ***Ask*** a question that begins with, "What if..."
- ***Leader***, remain quiet and listen.

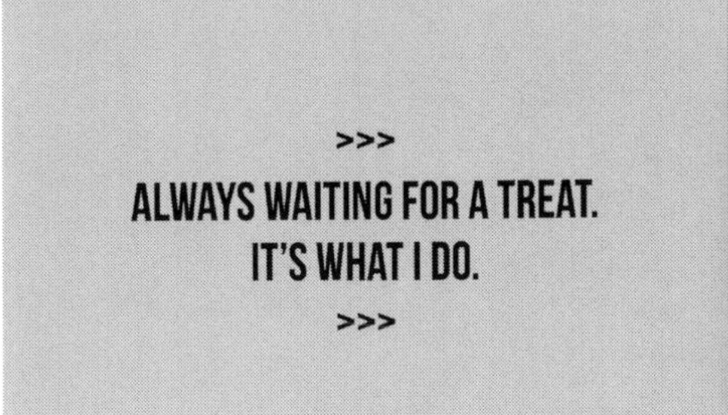

- *Brainstorm*—write down all the ideas on a white board. Give people ample time to ponder and discuss.
- *Review* all possibilities and decide on a path of growth together. You may decide the way you've done it IS the best way at this point, but at least you'll have more buy in.
- *Accountability* is the key to keeping trust alive and following through on getting things done.

I know this takes time and effort, but the loss of creativity and teamwork has a much greater cost on productivity, efficiency, and profitability for the organization as a whole. Breaking through the barrier of WADITW is freeing and breeds a culture of trust, thereby increasing engagement.

While Louie likes his comfortable habits, he also exudes excitement when I change things up for him. He can sense my enthusiasm, and he trusts that whatever adventure I am willing to go on, will be good for him.

5.8

YOU CAN'T MAKE ME SOMETHING I DON'T WANT TO BE!

Empowered to change

Louie was not having it. He planted all four paws on the floor and would not move an inch. His face let me know he was not pleased. At all. "Louie," I said sternly as I tried to squeeze his 40 pounds of muscle where it didn't want to go. "This is only for two hours, if that. Surely you can oblige me."

I sat back and stared at him, exasperated. For the last few Halloweens, I've donned a Cruella de Vil look and spent the evening with my grandchildren. This year I thought it would be fun to take Louie along in a Dalmatian outfit. Except there were no Dalmatian costumes for dogs. The closest thing I could find was a child's costume for a spotted cow.

I had imagined how it would turn out. I knew Louie would not share my enthusiasm for this creative costume. But I was counting on him forgetting all about it when he set eyes on my granddaughters, Evi and Mea. He'd jump out of the car and happily trot with them along the street, greeting other children, trying to get a peek into their candy loot. I just knew Louie would have more fun than he could imagine if he could just push through wearing a silly cow outfit and look as much like a Dalmatian as he could.

I also imagined it would make a great blog lesson: all about pressing through uncomfortable situations to enjoy the outcome. Sounds good, right?

But none of that happened. Yes, Lou was happy to see Evi and Mea. He did enjoy it when other children came up to love on him. But he hated his costume and was mad at me the entire time. He wouldn't even pose for a picture, and believe me, that's not like him.

I finally took the costume off and let him be Louie.

Too often we find ourselves being something we don't want to be. Maybe it's of our own doing—because we think we need to fit in, and it requires being someone "different." But often it's because someone else expects us to be different than what we are.

Maybe it's a negative thing: a boss requires us to be something based on their own insecurities. Or maybe it's positive: a leader sees potential in us that we don't see or can even imagine, and they want to coach us to be better.

No matter the reason, we resist because it is uncomfortable to be something we are not. We don't want to don a costume and fake it.

It's tough to balance being authentic and, at the same time, develop beyond mediocrity toward excellence. It can feel like donning a facade and "faking it till we make it." What should leaders do to help folks grow?

If you're in a position of leadership, you can suggest someone continue to develop. You can provide tools, mentoring, and ongoing training. But you can't make them be something they don't want to be. Each person is responsible for taking that first step towards wanting to make significant changes in their lives.

Still, there are ways to influence those in whom you see potential. For example:

1. Watch to see whether the person shows an eagerness to learn and grow, i.e., reading books and asking for help.
2. Ask them where they see themselves going. What is their end goal?
3. Share with them what potential you see in them.
4. Be sure your expectations align with their skillset and desires.
5. If their end goal and desires outweigh their skillset, place them on a realistic development plan and be clear about expectations.

When Louie and I arrived back home, he was one tired pup. He slinked upstairs to his little bed for a good night's rest. His expression told me he was still traumatized by the costume. But as I knelt down to give him a kiss, I looked into his eyes and saw a little spark.

It was a look that said, "If you are trying to make me be something different than who I am, at least make me a lion!"

And with that, he tucked his head into the fold of his front paw and fell fast asleep. No doubt, that evening he dreamt of being a lion.

HOW TO JUST BE

I was sitting outside working on my computer; writing, emailing, information gathering, compiling reports—all the necessary tasks for an entrepreneur. It was a beautiful morning, and I was feeling quite proud of my productivity. During my flurry of activity, I noticed one constant being that didn't flinch the entire time I was working—Louie!

It wasn't that he was asleep and not moving, he was laying down and fully awake. Sometimes he'd gaze into the trees, looking for some creature that dared to walk across his kingdom…but not this time. He was just being! He was serenely experiencing every bit of beauty that nature offered. I have no doubt that he thought it was all for his pleasure alone.

As I watched him, I couldn't help but think, "It must be nice to be my dog and relax on the deck while I work to provide a nice home and good food." Then I had to laugh. Louie was teaching me a lesson that took me years to grasp and yet is still so easy to forget—how to just be. We get caught up in the "More" mode: I've got to do more, work more, network more, socialize more, Facebook more, more, more, more. Help—let me off this merry-go-round!

I'm not sure what Louie was thinking as he quietly enjoyed nature, but he inspired me to close my computer and experience the stillness as well. Ahhh, there it was, something I had been missing—peacefulness. Most of us never take the time to practice being still and emptying our minds of the stuff that clutters our thinking and clouds our wellbeing. The ability to just *be* is crucial to our ability to lead well.

There is an assumption that sitting quietly means you're not doing anything. But that may be our most productive time of creativity or processing a difficult issue...or praying about how to respond to something.

Recently, my peacefulness was disturbed by an offense against someone who is close to me. While my initial reaction was to clear up the wrong and let everyone know the information being spread was a lie, I decided to do what Louie does and just be. I took a few moments to process, and I did not jump on social media to see what all the craziness was about. I actually practiced being still and not reacting out of indignant anger. Instead, I focused my energy on encouraging the person who was wronged. I know that, given time, the truth always prevails.

I know another leader who demonstrated the leadership quality of "being." Ken Blanchard and Phil Hodges, who wrote *Lead Like Jesus,* shared the five habits of Jesus. The first one is Solitude: "Jesus modeled solitude as an integral, strategic component of His leadership. In solitude and prayer, away from the hopes and hurts of those who looked to him with high and compelling expectations, Jesus again received instructions on the best use of the next day from God." This also gave Jesus the strength to stand up to others who gossiped, mocked, and eventually crucified him. He didn't draw a sword nor did he spew angry words, yet His quiet spirit shook people to the very core of their being. Now that's power!

Just *being* is necessary for us to make good decisions that positively affect our lives and those around us. Be intentional about being still.

5.10

WALK WITH CONFIDENCE

I've noticed something a bit different lately about Louie, my rescue pup. He really enjoys it when we walk side by side during our walks. What's different about that, you might ask?

He's always enjoyed our time together and is usually all over the place when we walk. To get him to walk right next to me (as we've been taught during dog training), I usually have to make him heel. What's different now is that he heels without me giving the command. Now he walks right next to me, many times for the entire walk, enjoying every step. It's like we're BFFs just hanging out. Well, maybe we are, but this change in our walks together gives me *paws* to think about leadership.

Louie walks next to me with confidence and joy because I, his leader, am walking with confidence and joy. This time last year I was still recuperating from a terrible accident. And, needless to say, this winter, though I was out walking, I walked with extreme caution. Now that the weather is turning warmer, there's a bit more spring in my step and I am back to walking confidently and fast. And Louie is reaping the benefits.

When I say, "Leader, you must walk with confidence," it may conjure up a lot of different thoughts and feelings about leadership. Many leaders walk with confidence because of pride issues, others put on airs and act like they're confident. I believe the leaders who truly are confident provide a safe place for employees to flourish. Those leaders are confident, not in their own abilities, but in the abilities and strengths of those they lead. They can walk with confidence because they

have a team around them they believe in, one they have encouraged and affirmed, and they work well together.

Walking with confidence is not about you, it is about those you lead, those you've empowered to be who they were created to be. It's not about you puffing yourself up, it's about those who choose to follow you and the confidence they have in you to be an excellent leader. Take the challenge and walk with confidence, but be sure it is because of the outward focus you have on the strengths and skills of others on your team.

As for Louie, well, I'm pretty sure if he were writing this it would be all about his confidence and how he walks next to me to make sure I am protected. Way to go, Louie! Such a good boy!

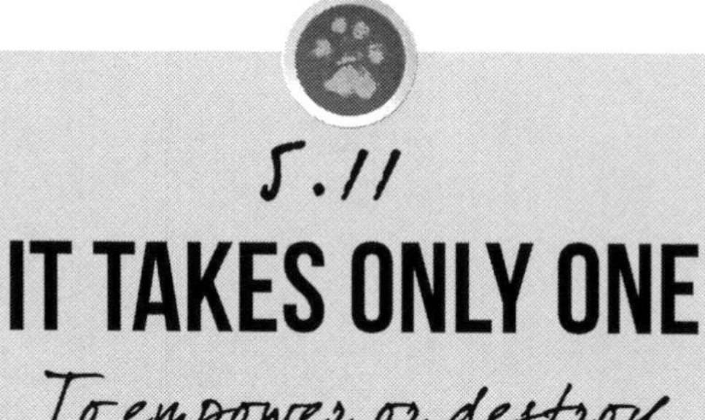

5.11

IT TAKES ONLY ONE

To empower or destroy

Louie and I were enjoying an evening stroll in our neighborhood and stopped to talk to several neighbors. As we finished one conversation, Louie picked up the pace to continue our walk when suddenly, from out of nowhere, another dog charged him, barking feverishly.

Louie's first reaction to any threat, real or imagined, is to run as fast as he can. But being on a leash prohibits that reaction, so he resorts to his next natural reaction: to fight. Louie's hackles went up immediately, and he bared his teeth and growled viciously.

Never mind that the threat was an elderly, twelve-pound pug named Sophie who had gotten loose from her owner. Leash and all, she went after Louie with all her might. I yanked on Louie's leash and commanded him to stop. But how could I do that when his very life was being threatened (or so he thought)? Sophie's owner stood back and did not come to the rescue. Here I was telling my dog not to react while hers was loose and giving Louie all she had. When I realized I would not get any help from her owner, I reached down, grabbed Sophie, and in my best imitation of Clint Eastwood, hissed in her ear, "Not with my dog, you don't!"

I handed Sophie over to her owner, and Louie and I continued walking, a bit out of breath but glad to be away from the nuisance. I was ticked, to say the least. In the heat of the moment, I thought of letting Louie do whatever he wanted to that little Sophie, but decided not to allow the situation to escalate. It seemed unfair that I told my dog not to behave badly yet he was the one being attacked.

Oh, gee, wait . . . we do that all the time in our organizations, don't we? Someone attacks another, and we stand by and watch because the attacker is "harmless" (or so we think). We try to handle the better-behaved employee because they take feedback well and are more apt to listen. Meanwhile, the attacker continues down their path of destruction. Many times, we don't want to confront the attacker because of the havoc they will wreak. We brush off such poor behavior, reasoning that the attacker either didn't mean any harm or must have had an issue outside of that they're struggling to handle. After all, they really are a nice person, right?

Right! Sophie's an adorable dog—unless you're another dog and happen to be anywhere in her sight!

Now, I know there is a theory about why small dogs think they need to go after larger dogs. I've owned a few of those small dogs myself; the most notorious was Cece. My sister, Mary Jo, described her as scrappy. Cece would chase after the Rottweiler down the street. The bigger the dog, the more aggressively Cece would take it on. So embarrassing! But Cece and the small dog syndrome is a whole other topic.

This chapter is about how it takes only one person to destroy a team and set it back. Louie was skittish on walks after that incident with one little dog, which seemed to set us back years to when I first adopted him and he was filled with fear. Sophie behaved poorly, Louie was reprimanded, and we found ourselves back at square one.

By the same token, it takes only one person to

1. Change a culture.
2. Influence team members for the greater good.
3. Cast the vision for a team.
4. Move a team toward the next part of the journey.
5. Do the right thing (think of the movie *12 Angry Men*).

6. Confront the office or neighborhood bully.
7. Model love, kindness, trust, and respect.
8. Refuse to give in when faced with what seems like a setback.

Louie and Sophie will never be friends, but he should at least not have to fear her as we walk down the street. In reflecting on this situation, I've set out to be that one person who can positively affect others' lives despite those who do nothing but attack. I encourage you to do the same and, perhaps collectively, we can make our world a better place.

5.12

THE CONE OF SHAME

The need to adapt

When Louie had to have surgery to remove the growth on his paw, it was a pretty quick decision, with some uncertainty about what the growth was and how he would handle the recuperation period. He survived the surgery well, and the growth was a papilloma, a wart. The biggest issue we had was keeping him away from the stitches. Louie is like Houdini; he can get out of any bandage or covering that I put on him to prevent him from chewing on his paw. I was amazed at how many times I found his bandage on the floor somewhere.

We came home with a very nice, pliable, see-through cone that was to be placed over his head to keep him from chewing his stitches. I was hesitant to use it because of the look he gave me when I tried to put it on him. First, it was a look of defiance (gee, I've never seen that one before), and then he'd look as though I was trying to kill him. And finally, I'd get the puppy-dog-big-brown eyes that captured my heart the very first time I met him.

I attached his collar and slid the cone over his head, stating in a serious, parental tone, "This is for your own good, buddy." He hated it! And he was mad at me. He decided the best thing he could do was trot out of the room and go to his happy place to look out the window and be away from me. Except he ran into the doorframe and stopped. He looked back at me with a look of "Are you kidding me?" Then he set himself back on track, maneuvered the cone to clear the doorframe, and walked out of the room.

Next, he hit the doorframe going into the room with a view. Again he stopped, looked back at me, and shook his head. Again he set himself back on track and maneuvered the cone so he could walk into the room, clearing the doorframe. I could hear him trying to jump up on the seat to look out the window, but because the cone got in the way, he fell back down. He tried again, missed again, and fell back down.

I resisted the urge to jump in and help. I knew he could do it; he just needed to adjust himself a bit to clear the seat. And so he did, finally, and then positioned himself as close to the window as possible so that everyone could see him and would feel sorry for him. And they did.

I learned a few valuable leadership lessons thanks to the cone of shame:

1. As tough as it was for him to wear, it helped in the healing process.
2. In order to achieve a goal (look out the window), he had to make several adjustments and think outside the "cone."
3. As a leader, you can't always jump in to rescue someone. In order to truly empower them, they have to learn things for themselves, as tough as it is to watch them fall.
4. Louie learned a few new things; like how to eat his food with the cone, even though he looked like a vacuum cleaner as he leaned over his bowl and inhaled.
5. He figured out pretty quickly that he was good at tipping the water bowl over.

6. There was no need for me to walk around calling the contraption on his head the cone of shame. Well, actually, that's a lie—he hated it and no doubt, was ashamed to wear it!
7. The less opportunity he had to bother his stitches, the faster he healed and the longer the cone stayed off. For Louie, this meant that he felt better, and was back to taking walks and playing with his pals.

Louie soaked in the attention for as long as he could. As time passed and his stitches were removed, I realized the overarching lesson of this entire experience.

While we must take time to heal from some of life's tough lessons, deep down inside, we know we can adjust and adapt. And in that perseverance, we may actually learn to enjoy life more.

5.13

THE FINAL CHAPTER

Life interrupted

December 18, 2016 was filled with great anticipation. It was one week before Christmas, and the DiStasi family was planning to gather at my house to celebrate Christmas. Everything was set: the massive amounts of food, the decorations, gifts, and music. It was to be a celebration to top all the ones we had celebrated so far as a family.

Louie and I took our usual stroll early that morning. Two days before, there had been a late evening ice storm, but this particular morning seemed okay as far as icy pavement was concerned. Still, I was cautious and walked in the grass as much as possible.

An elderly neighbor has a very long driveway, and Louie and I had been taking her daily newspaper to her so she would not have to venture out and lean over to pick it up. As soon as I stepped on the driveway, my feet flew up in the air, and I landed on my left hip. I lost control of Louie, and it took me a few moments to catch my breath. I couldn't see Louie, and panic was about to set in. His normal reaction when something startles him is to run away. And seeing his mama flying through the air had to have been startling.

I forced myself to turn as far to the left as I could. There Louie sat, close behind my left shoulder. I reached around to draw him close to me. As he tucked his head under my arm, I felt his shaking and heard him whimper. To hear him cry broke my heart, and my tears started to flow uncontrollably. I knew I could not move—and whatever would take place from that moment forward, it would be a long journey. Louie chose to stay by me as the faithful, truly empowered, loyal friend that he is.

A neighbor pulled up with his phone in hand, already calling 911, and I called my friend and neighbor Cindy to pick up Louie. I called my daughter, Marisa, and the network of community, family, and friends jumped into action. Everyone's life was interrupted on December 18, 2016.

After a jarring ambulance ride, surgery to repair a femur that was fractured in two places, a total hip replacement, five days in the hospital, and physical therapy, I was released to Marisa and Matt's home for respite care and to celebrate Christmas with the two cutest nurses on the face of the earth. Louie had been well taken care of by my wonderful neighbors who had walked him, let him stay in their homes, taken him to daycare to play, and given him more love than he could imagine.

Life interrupted has taught Louie and me a few things:

1. **We appreciate life and the little things.** Although that seems so cliché, it was the small steps of accomplishment that filled me with joy. Every day, I set new goals to accomplish—goals I never would have dreamed to set before. For instance, I learned to get out of bed, to go to the bathroom, to take my meds without having to wake my daughter to help me, and to carry a cup of coffee

>>>

THE CUTEST NURSES EVER

>>>

in the morning to enjoy my quiet time. Mea and Evi helped me do things as they watched me improve. Christmas had a deeper meaning that year with sincere thankfulness, love, and joy!

2. **You really do know who your friends are.** So many people dropped everything to help. It was a terrible strain on Marisa and Matt as they took care of me. So many friends offered to grocery shop, run errands, and stay with me when I finally came home. My sisters and cousin packed their clothes and took turns staying overnight. My brothers were calling, visiting, and bringing food. The neighbors who took care of Louie were such Godsends. Many people could not help because of logistics, but they checked in and prayed.
3. **You have to move out of your comfort zone.** This was a tough one for Louie and me. I had to let people help me. What a humbling position to be in; I was helpless. I have never stayed in a hospital other than to give birth. I don't take any medicines, and I have never fractured a single bone. The outpouring of love and encouragement was overwhelming. Louie had to be comfortable with people coming and going in and out of our home and driving him to and from daycare. But we both pressed on through pain, frustration, fear, and being uncomfortable. It was difficult, but we made it past the hardest part of this process. There will always be a next move out of our comfort zone. I have no doubt we'll press through that too.
4. **Some things just do not matter.** The superficiality of the holidays clashed with the richness of genuine, loving relationships. There can be no comparison of the things that are bought with the things that are sought, caught, and taught. The characteristics of love, joy, and peace are important for us to live and pass on to others. It takes effort, but it is worth the time and effort. I am a better person because of the love, joy, and peace that others shared with me during that season.

This year, as every year should be, is going to be a great year of love and strength. Louie is a better dog because he chose faithfulness over running away. He trusted and allowed others into his world to help us! We are closer because of those tough few weeks. Thank you to so many for being in my life and for your prayers and support!

BACK TO NORMAL, WHATEVER THAT MEANS!

Louie was as traumatized as I was, through the journey of falling and consequent surgery. He had to adjust to my being gone for two weeks; friends coming and going, walking and feeding him, playing with him, all while he constantly watched the door with the hope I would walk through it any minute.

Once I was home, he learned to trust my erratic movements with a cane and settled back into some interesting habits: growling at people who come to my door (even his dog walkers) and jumping on the couch to sit directly across from me (better to watch me, he says).

One evening, a friend came by to take Louie for a walk. After they finished and she came in to sit with me for awhile, he ran into the house, checked on me, and then ran upstairs, where he ran the length of the hallway several times. Then, I heard a big commotion, and from where I was sitting, I could tell what that little rascal was doing. He was getting into my clothesbasket in my bathroom and taking all the clothes out of it, having no consideration whatsoever for the amount of time it took me to get the clothes into that basket.

His continued motion, which was evident even though he was a floor above me, indicated he not only removed the items from the basket, he was also rolling in them—all of them! Some time ago I explained to Zig, our trainer, Louie's annoying bad habit of rolling in the dirty laundry. I assumed it was because he wanted to surround himself with my smell, weird as that is.

But Zig assured me that was not it at all. Louie was getting his smell on my clothes, showing his dominance over me. WHAT? Now that is a really annoying bad habit that makes me realize we are back to square one. There will be no dominance of Louie over me.

But this is not surprising. When it takes all my energy to walk from the living room to the kitchen, disciplining a dog is not high on my list, especially since we've been through this before. The pressure was off of Louie to behave well, and when the pressure is off, he reverts back to his old habits.

That is so like us. As stated in a previous chapter, one dynamic of change is that when the pressure is off, we revert to our original behaviors. Well, the pressure was definitely off, and Louie was back to some of his old habits. We would have to spend time correcting that. But rather than lament, I reflected on what this means as far as my recent journey and getting "back to normal."

Finally being able to drive did give me a sense of life getting back to normal. Getting off medication, walking better, and looking forward to some normalcy were great goals for recovery. But did I really want normalcy to be my goal?

Not this time, not this year. I am going to be intentional (keeping the pressure on) about breaking past the norm to live a well-meaning life by doing the following:

1. Pruning activities, objects, and even some relationships, all to devote precious time to what matters.
2. Being kind in thought, word, and deed, whether people deserve it or not. I don't mean just merely being nice (and sometimes superficial and phony), but being authentic and loving—speaking truth in love and showing those

>>>
DANCING THE NIGHT AWAY!
>>>

who differ from me, or have differing viewpoints, the compassion that only comes from faith.

3. Taking time to listen in order to learn—and not rushing to the next project.
4. Being still and having plenty of margin in my life.
5. Laughing more.
6. Dancing (okay, that one is normal for me, but now takes on an even more special meaning). I will take time to dance more with my grandchildren and even my adult daughter, because that's what DiStasi kids do. My niece, Sara, was married in 2017, and she promised we would dance the night away if I was back to normal. And dance the night away we did!

Be intentional about breaking past the norm. Life is too short and too easily interrupted for us to stay stuck in the status quo. And you are never too old to take that first step to crashing through the "same ol', same ol'."

As for Louie, we have some work to do. As I have been writing, he slipped into my laundry room and pulled out a dishtowel. He is so bad. I know he has a large fan base of people who love him, but this annoying little habit just makes me shake my head. I suppose being intentionally kind will be continual with little Louie DiStasi!

AUTHOR'S NOTE

Thank you for taking the time to read *Lead Like Louie.* While this completes our book, the lessons continue with Louie's blogs. Lead Like Louie can be found by going to our webpage, di-advisors.com, and click on the banner for the blog, or go to louieleads.com.

The **LOUIE/PAWS** Leadership model provides a simple method to lead, whether you're CEO of a large corporation, an entrepreneur with five employees, a teacher, pastor, parent, or student. The steps are simple, but are not necessarily easy.

I. **LOVE:** This is the toughest step to intentionally walk out. It takes strength to love others, especially when we don't like them very much or when they annoy us. A true leader is one who can set aside differences, speak truth in love and with boldness, and serve others. This is foundational in building a culture of trust.

II. **OBJECTIVES and GOALS:** People need to know what direction they are going. They need vision and goals that keep them on track. As leaders, it is important to provide specific guidance in order for people to use their strengths and gifts and flourish in their roles, which results in productivity, profitability, and an overall sense of value.

III. **UNDERSTANDING OTHERS:** This is where we humans run into problems, and where we can learn so much from our pets. They unconditionally love and their single goal in life is to please their humans. And sadly, I believe they understand humans much better than humans do. There are a number of reasons for our misunderstanding other humans. In our speeches and workshops, we go into this information in much greater detail:

a. Miscommunication based on our body language, tone of voice and words.
b. We all process information differently.
c. We all have stuff and emotional baggage in our background.
d. We're all at different levels of understanding and development.

When we do run into an issue of misunderstanding, the **PAWS** method is the best tool to use to handle conflict:

a. **Pause:** Stop, take a breath, think!
b. **Ask** yourself what is going on, why am I upset, how can I help, etc.
c. **Wisdom:** Choose your words carefully, always choose wisdom.
d. **Stop and Seek** to understand: Take time to understand the other's point of view.

IV. **INVEST IN OTHERS:** It takes time to lead. It will not happen overnight. We need to invest our time, talents, and treasures into other people to help develop them. It is never about who we are as leaders, it is about who we develop and how much time we take to do so. This is critical before our last step.

IV. **EMPOWER OTHERS:** Most leaders jump to this stage too quickly. If you do not love your employees, set up goals and help them to achieve them, understand who they are as humans, and invest time in them, it is a disservice to empower them. Once you have gone through all the stages, this last step is the most loving. Empowering others, employees, children, etc., is key to their ongoing development.

The LOUIE/PAWS model is critical to our leadership style and ongoing development of others. Each step should be reviewed each week in your one-on-one meetings. Leaders should commit to reviewing this information on a regular basis, it is not a one-time shot.

Louie has changed thanks to my using this model over and over again. He has learned to trust me and, for the most part, has removed fear from his life because of that trust. This model works with our human relationships, but the key is intentionality. You have to work this plan in order for it to work.

We hope this is the beginning of a renewed leadership model that benefits you personally and professionally, as well as those around you. DiStasi Advisors is committed to seeing others be the relational leaders they were created to be.

Thank you, and many blessings.

—Danise and Louie

ABOUT MY PET, DANISE

Danise C. DiStasi adopted her rescue dog, Louie, in 2013 in Cincinnati, where she grew up. In addition to being an author, DiStasi is a noted speaker, Executive Coach, and workshop facilitator. After graduating from Xavier University with a degree in radiologic science, she spent twenty-seven years in the medical industry. Her positions over that time ranged from nuclear product specialist to manager and vice president of sales and marketing.

In 2001, DiStasi began focusing on a career in business development and training when she joined the Ken Blanchard Companies. Currently, she is president and chief relationship officer of DiStasi Advisors LLC, where she has been coaching and consulting since 2005. Her clients have included Fortune 500 C-level executives and their teams, whom she has coached on leadership, character development, productivity, performance, and team-building solutions. Danise has two grandchildren, and enjoys time with her family, gardening, and spending time with Louie.

Made in the USA
Middletown, DE
25 June 2019